#SPEAKING POTION

#SPEAKING POTION

mastering the art of public speaking

COLBY SYLVAIN

Printed in the United States of America
The Union Family Publishing

To order additional copies of this title, contact your favorite local bookstore

Print Edition ISBN: 978-1-61468-530-2
Digital Edition ISBN: 978-1-61468-531-9

· CONTENTS ·

• DEDICATION •

Speaking Potion is dedicated to my mother, Marie Alette Dorcena, better known as, Marie Mention. I pray God give you strength to overcome chemotherapy and become cancer free. As a token of my appreciation for all you've done for me, all the proceeds from the sells of Speaking Potion will go towards paying off your mortgage so that you may finally get a chance to enjoy retirement. You've dedicated your life to taking care of others while working as a nurses aid, and on behalf of all your patients, Thank You. Thank you for showing me that life is about helping others. May the contents in this book help everyone that needs it.

Love Your #1 Son,
Colby Sylvain

To everyone out there that has a fear of speaking in public, don't stop fighting to overcome your fear. There are messages within you that others need to hear in order for our world to become a better place. Share your experiences to help enlighten those that are in the dark. By letting your light shine, you unconsciously give others around you the inspiration and motivation to do the same. Thank you for pur-chasing Speaking Potion.

Together We Overcome Struggles,
Colby Sylvain

· INTRODUCTION ·

IN YOU IS THE WORLD'S GREATEST PUBLIC SPEAKER!
There were many before you, but *you* are the only one that matters. Hi, I'm Colby Sylvain, and I was compelled to write this book especially for *you*. If you believe in the laws of attraction, then you will understand me when I tell you that this book is the missing piece to your public speaking puzzle. The energies I've placed into writing this book are meant to be mentally absorbed. The information obtained will give you such a great purpose in life that the stagnation of *your* fear of speaking in public will be one of the last obstacles in becoming the extraordinary person *you* were created to be.

Thank you for choosing me as your partner in this transformation that you are about to make. Believe it or not, I was placed here for this very purpose: to help you understand this simple formula that has worked for me. Before I could effectively be of service to you, I went through certain similar situations to better understand what it is that I was sent to do. Like you, perhaps, I was the quiet student in class that didn't like raising his hand to answer questions, whether I knew the answer or not. I didn't want everyone's attention on me. I hated the sound of my voice, hated my limited vocabulary, and hated being in the spotlight. I was one who didn't like being in crowded places, the one who'd remained silent when the question was asked: "Does anyone else have anything to say?" I was the one with a whole lot to say, but wouldn't let it out because I was shy. I hated the idea of having to say *anything* in public.

"Just leave me the hell alone!" was my mentality. Silence was my best friend; solitude was my heaven. My life came to a point where I had isolated myself from everyone. I'd much rather be around animals. But that was until I became aware of a major problem in my community and developed a passion for wanting to help the people there by creating a solution.

The problem was a lack of self-confidence. Seeing lack of self-confidence in the people around me helped me to also see it in myself. I came to the realization that, for years, I've cheated myself out of achieving all of the successful things that life has to offer. It wasn't until I began to realize this false sense of fear was the reason for all my insecurities that change began. In school, although I might have known the answers, my self-confidence was too low to transmit the energy from my brain to my arm to make it rise. The reason why I hated to be around groups of people was because my self-confidence level was so low that I placed everyone else above me. Instead of feeding off of their energy, I felt inferior to them.

I allowed myself to believe whatever I had to say wasn't worth listening to. I became my worst critic. The reason why? I was never passionate about *anything* enough to ever want to re-wire the connections that controlled my self-confidence. It took me forty years to understand and realize that without passion for the problems of the people, there is no progress. Once I came upon this realization, I took the necessary steps towards building my self-confidence by facing my fear of speaking in public. Would you like to know how I did it?

I joined a theater workshop and took part in a play called "This Is This." Once the play was done, I joined a public speaking class, sponsored by Toastmasters International, to learn the fundamentals of speaking in public. You're probably wondering, "Why did you take part in a play and *then* join a public speaking class?" Well, I'll tell you why later. For now, I want to speak to you on two very important topics pertaining to overcoming your fear of public speaking. One is the effectiveness of the three Ps: people, problems, and passions. Second is the power of believing in yourself.

Using the three Ps, you can analyze your surroundings and come up with an intelligible solution for helping people with their problems. People are the most valuable resource there is in the world. This means we are all valuable and capable of doing something that can help us generate some form of financial stability. There are problems all around us. No matter where we go in the world, we are bound to come across some sort of problem people are facing. It doesn't always have to be your own problem, but a problem in general. For example, if you go to Africa, you will find that many of its countries have problems with water systems, food shortages, untreated diseases (due to lack of medicine), electricity, education, and transportation, to name a few; however, what a lot of people fail to understand is that there are many organizations, and corporations, that are profiting from these problems. Some are providing humanitarian services, others are there for their own self-interest.

In situations like these, the companies that comes there to make a profit usually don't last long. The ones that last are passionate about making a difference. They become the most successful because when someone's intention is to help others, they will always benefit in the long run. It's karma. You reap what you sow. Having the passion to help people with their problems will produce profits—but you have to believe in what you are doing and believe that you are the right person to be doing it.

When I took on the acting job, I believed that I was the right person to play the character. Believing in myself was what kept me going even after some friends of mine suggested I quit. In my heart and mind, I believed if I didn't go through with the play, it would have made me a coward. This was a problem that I developed a passion for proving otherwise. And by facing that fear, I developed a passion for public speaking. Once I was able to take a public speaking class where I got to write a speech, I used the opportunity to write about a topic that I am passionate about: bullyism.

You can read the speech "Time To Rise" at the end of the book, along with a few interviews I conducted with some extremely talented public speakers who I met during my journey. I transformed being a person who had a fear of speaking in public to participating in a play, receiving a certificate, and writing a book on public speaking. As you will see from the date on my public speaking class certificate, all of this happened within a very short time span. I believe if you follow the advices in *Speaking Potion*, you will accomplish your goal.

I put my heart into writing this book, and as I'm writing it I prayed for guidance before starting each chapter. So what you're getting is not only informational, but spiritual too. My message is purely from my very own experiences. When I ask you to *understand* in chapter one, it is because without understanding their can't be any growth. I had to understand why I wanted to overcome my fear of public speaking in order to boldly face the challenges ahead that eventually helped me to grow.

When I tell you to *watch, listen, and learn* in chapter two, it is because that is what I had to do in order for me to get to where I currently am with my knowledge of public speaking. *The copycat effect* that I mention in chapter three is a tool you will come to use. You will understand why it's effective and how it can help you develop and enhance your style of speaking. *Talking your talk* from chapter four is the key to becoming a confident public speaker.

In chapter five, you will learn the importance of *converting your passion*. This passion will give you the drive to achieve financial, emotional, spiritual, and physical freedom. If you want to see what a passion-filled person does, you can go watch QVC on the Home Shopping Network to see clothing designer Susan Graver maneuver in an effortless fashion. Or, if you're a sports person, you can watch ESPN and hear Steven A. Smith, Molly Qerim, and Max Kellerman go at it with such intensity that you would think they're enemies.

In chapter six, I will cover the importance of being a worldly person so that you can *recognize your audience* and know what they want and don't want. Chapter seven will provide you with some basic tools to *control your lips*. You will learn why breathing right is essential to your career as a public speaker. In chapter eight, I will explain why you should *align with your sign*. Your horoscope sign is filled with information that you need to know about yourself. Find out who you are connected to, and how to achieve equal success.

Chapter nine is all about you and how to put yourself first in everything that you do. *Being the "I" in team* will show you how to use what you've learned from others to better yourself. Next we're going to get inside your *tool shed* in chapter ten. You'll be surprised how valuable some of your life experiences may be. By now you should've learned enough to be ready for chapter eleven, so *let's write a speech*. Are you able to show that you understand everything you've learned? If so use all of the methods from each chapter to write a speech. You can make the speech about anything. In chapter twelve, I just have one last message for you: *the world is yours*. That's right, the world is your stage. Make sure every time you step onto stage, you are prepared.

Oh! Don't worry about trying to stay focused. I'm going to make this a fun journey for you. As I share with you my formula to become a great public speaker, I'm going to introduce you to two of my buddies: Jen and Joe. They'll entertain you through this oh-so-wonderful experience. Have fun, and remember to take advantage of every speaking opportunity. Let your truth be your potion each and every time you are speaking.

· PROLOGUE ·

Joe James Johnson is at home on the internet promoting his book *Speaking Potion* on Instagram. Suddenly his iPhone rings, filling the room with the sound of Justin Bieber's latest hit. Glancing down at the screen, Joe notices it's his friend, Jennifer Juliet Jackson, calling. Sensing it may be urgent, since Jen doesn't usually call this late. he picks up.

Joe: "Hey, Jen. What's going on?"

Jen: "Joe, I need your help."

Joe: "What's up, Jen Juice, what's the problem? You know I'll do almost anything for you."

Jen: "You know how I always tell you that you talk too much?"

Joe: "Yeah?"

Jen: "Well, I need you to teach me how to do it."

Joe: "Do what, Jen?"

Jen: "Talk too much."

Joe: "Talk too much?"

Jen: "Yeah. I just received an offer to be the spokesperson for Vain Apparel. I'll be getting paid to represent the brand throughout the world. I was told I would be responsible for giving presentations—"

Joe: "Presentations!"

Jen: "Yeah, you know. Giving speeches in rooms filled with

strangers, doing commercials, interviews. They're paying $30,000 for every presentation I do."

Joe: "Wow! $30,000 is a lot of money. So, what's the problem?"

Jen: "The problem is I have a terrible fear of public speaking. I can communicate just fine with one, two, or even three people. Any more than that I *lose it.*"

Joe: "What do you mean? How do you lose it?"

Jen: "Well, for starters, I get nervous, embarrassed. I start sweating. Oh my God! I sweat so much you would think I came out of a sauna. I forget what I want to say and how I want to say it. I stumble on my words. I start to think that everyone is laughing at me. I get real uncomfortable."

Joe: "Well if public speaking is your problem, Jen, I have the solution."

Jen: "I knew you would, Joe. That's why I called you."

Joe: "Did you try my speaking potion?"

Jen: "Speaking potion?"

Joe: "Yeah, *Speaking Potion.* My book? Wait a minute. Jen, you haven't read it, have you?"

Jen: "I—huh—well—wait a sec. Why potion?"

Joe: "A potion is a mixture of liquids, right?"

Jen: "Yeah."

Joe: "To become a great public speaker, you have to use a mixture of speech, gestures, props, stories, quotes, and so on. It takes fifty-six percent body language, thirty-seven percent tone of voice, and seven percent words."

Jen: "Ohhhh, I get it."

Joe: "Guess you never got my book then, huh?"

Jen: "I—I...."

Joe: "Didn't you receive the free copy I sent you?"

Jen: "I meant to read it, but I've been so busy."

Joe: "And now you need the skills for your new job. I would suggest you go read it."

Jen: "Okay, now I remember. I gave it to Kloeh for her birthday."

Joe: "So you re-gifted my gift? Is that what you're telling me?"

Jen: "Sorry, Joe. Would you mind reading it to me over the phone?"

Joe: "Do what?! Jen, I can't do—"

Jen: "Please, Joe. Pretty, pretty please with sugar on top."

Joe: "Putting sugar on top of the 'please' is not going to make me change my mind, Jen."

Jen: "Why not, Joe? Sugar is sweet."

Joe: "Exactly. And I'm a diabetic, in case you forgot."

Jen: "I'm sorry, Joe, I didn't mean to put any sugar on top of the 'please.' I'll take it back. What can I do to convince you to read *Speaking Potion* to me over the phone?"

Joe: "I should've made an audio version. You really want me to read it to you over the phone, Jen?"

Jen: "Yes, Joe, yes! I desperately need you to read it to me. I'm ready to take in everything you have to tell me."

Joe: "I'll tell you what. I'll read it to you, but when I'm done, I'm going to need you to do me a favor."

Jen: Anything, Joe, anything. You name it and I'll do it."

Joe: "Wow, you gave in pretty quickly. This job interview must mean the world to you, huh?"

Jen: "Oh, Joe, if you only knew. I've been waiting to get my foot in the door of the fashion world ever since my dad bought me an Alexander McQueen dress for my high school prom. It was one of the best nights of my life. I was even the envy of some of my teachers."

Joe: "I think you would have been the envy with or without that dress, Jen. Look at you. You're drop-dead gorgeous."

Jen: "Thanks, but I know you're only saying that because you're my friend."

Joe: "Your friend, your friend! No Jen, I'm more like your fan. I worship the ground that you walk on."

Jen: "Oh please, Joe. You see beautiful women every day in Brooklyn."

Joe: "Even if I do, it's obvious that none are like you because no matter how many different beautiful women I see, I still somehow can't stop thinking about *your* beauty."

Jen: "Stop it, Joe. You're making me blush. Plus, that's not why I called you, remember? I need to know how to overcome my fear of public speaking."

Joe: "Okay, okay, okay. I'll go get the book and we can get right to it. Does your phone have facetime?"

Jen: "No. Not the phone I'm using at the moment. My smart-phone does, but I just placed it on the charger."

Joe: "That's too bad."

Jen: "Why?"

Joe: "Because looking at your beautiful face while speaking to you would have put me in a better state of mind."

Jen: "But wouldn't that just be a distraction?"

Joe: "I can never be distracted by who I'm attracted to. If anything, looking at you would be my motivation."

Jen: "Well, I'll tell you what. How about I send you a selfie?"

Joe: "Or you can just come by, and we can read the book together."

Jen: "I would, but I'm already in bed. To get up and get dressed to come all the way to Brooklyn from Manhattan will take too much time, and I have to be up early tomorrow."

Joe: "No problem. But, if you change your mind later, you're always welcome to come by. Okay, here we go, I have the book with me now. I'm going to skip the introduction and start you off from chapter one."

· CHAPTER 1 ·

UNDERSTANDING

Understanding the importance of being a good public speaker is critical to becoming the most valuable asset in whatever field you are currently at in life. All aspects of the business world (and life) are about growth. As human beings, we must be able to effectively communicate with one another about anything that revolves around our survival and evolution. In every environment of the world you will encounter what I call the three Ps: people, problems, and passions. When a person understands the benefits of being a good public speaker, he or she is automatically propelled to a higher level of existence than others. Why?

Communication makes the world go around. Without us having the ability to communicate with one another, nothing would get done. The world would be a dull place to live. Since most great things must be done in a group setting, it will take people with the ability to speak in public to communicate with the masses. Since the beginning of time public speakers have been sought after to be the voice that passes on messages, carries on traditions. Having access to a public speaker back then was as good as having internet access now.

In the bible, God was the first to make use of a public speaker when he chose Abraham to be an conduit. By God choosing Abraham to help solve the people's problems, Abraham's life propelled to a high level of existence. He was then held at a higher standard than his fellow men. Any problems that occurred became Abraham's responsibility to solve. He became a leader to his people.

The reason why God gave Abraham this power was because Abraham was one of the only men with enough passion for the people's problems. Abraham wanted to make a difference, and God gave him the voice to do it. To this day it is evident that some of the world's greatest speakers are people that were passionate about solving some type of problem. Throughout history these great men and women's lives are recorded in books, audios, and videos, but most importantly in the consciousness of the people.

Martin Luther King Jr. was a great public speaker because he was passionate about solving the racism in America. John F. Kennedy was a great speaker because he was passionate about solving many problems in America, such as the Cold War, segregation, and equal pay for women. Former President Barack H. Obama was a great speaker because he was passionate about solving economic and health-care problems.

You see, these men were all at one time ordinary citizens living in a nation full of people with problems that needed to be solved/addressed. Had they not developed a passion for solving the problems of the people, there would have been no need for them to become public speakers; however, they understood the importance of being good public speakers, so they strived to become great at it. Through public speaking they were able to not only help the people, but themselves. This is what I want *you* to focus on in this book: understanding the importance of being a good public speaker so that *you* can help others and yourself to become *any-*

thing that you set your mind to. The ability to speak in public is like having a superpower for some, and that is why most people have a fear of public speaking. It's a fear of possessing power.

Have you ever met someone who is smart yet insecure? Or maybe you know someone who can't stop talking and is as dumb as a doorknob? Being able to speak in public is a superpower that most people naturally have, but they don't know how to use it effectively. Thank God for that because I believe if some of them knew they possessed this power, they would use it more for evil than good. The power to effectively speak in public is like being in possession of a nuclear weapon. Hopefully when *you* develop your public speaking superpower, you will use it for good and not evil. There are levels to being a public speaker.

Great public speakers have the power to command an audience's attention, appeal to their emotional feelings, and influence their thinking. Most people can be easily persuaded when you speak to their heart. As an effective speaker you can change the hearts, minds, and lives of families, communities, countries, and even the world (depending on the size of your platform and topic).

Wherever you encounter powerful men and women (no matter their differences), the one similarity you will always come across is the fact that these powerful individuals have a way with words. They are good, if not great, at public speaking. They know how to engage, motivate, inspire, transform, and captivate their audience with their speech. Whether dictators like Fidel Castro and Kim Jong-un or dignitaries like Pope John Paul II and Toussaint L'Ouverture, speaking in front of large crowds is a mandatory requirement, for anyone who wishes to be on top of the ladder of success. The bigger the crowd you are able to control, the bigger your bank roll. As you are reading this, there are people that are getting paid hundreds of thousands of dollars to speak in front of business executives, college students, and so forth.

Would you like to become one of those people that are getting paid to speak in public? You already *are* one of those people—you just don't know it yet. Why don't you know it? Because you haven't discovered your *speaking potion*. You haven't studied the sweet science of successful speaking. Don't worry. By the time you're done absorbing and retaining all of this information, you will be ready, willing, and able to not only apply it to your life, but to pass it on to your loved ones so they, too, can become successful at speaking in public. This skill can open many doors to opportunities and build careers.

Right now, how much are your public speaking skills worth? If you were given free access to an empty football stadium for one night only and got paid one dollar per person that comes to hear you speak, how much money do you think you would make? What type of people would come to hear you speak? What would you be speaking about? How long do you think you would last discussing that topic?

No matter the amount of time you have, I can guarantee you'll make the most money by speaking on a topic that you are passionate about. This is the line that separates the rich dads from the poor dads, success from failure, winners from losers, easy-peasy life from hardknock life. It is so simple and so clear. Do you get it yet? If not, after I tell you what it is, please take a moment to think (deeply) about it: *Stick to what you know.* That is the basic element of understanding. When you stick to what *you* know, you can never fail, never lose, never be poor. We are all created with a survival gift. Everyone is born with a talent, a skill, a special gift.

A preacher preaches and becomes successful because that's what they know. A singer sings and becomes successful because singing is what they know. A sports caster gets paid to talk about sports because it's what they know. This rule applies to all walks of life. The things you don't know you can learn, and then it becomes what you know. If everyone sticks to doing what they know, life will be simple for all.

Unfortunately there are people in the world who don't place value in the things that they know. Therefore, those things tend to remain or become worthless. That is why it is so important for you to understand who *you* are and what *you* are worth. You have to love yourself to the point of understanding that *you* are an entity that is capable of providing the world with an essential service that is priceless. Your originality sets you apart from all others whom had come before you and done what you are about to do. Just like no two finger prints are the same, no two public speakers are the same. The uniqueness of your voice, look, style, and passion make you an interesting person to listen to.

I don't know whether you see it or not, but the world is heading in a direction where it's becoming easy for *anyone* to make a living out of simply being themselves. The internet has made it fashionable for unorthodox individuals to be accepted. You can see from the music we listen to and the types of TV shows we watch that things are constantly changing. Why? Because people are constantly changing things. Your voice can change the realm of public speaking. I believe the true reason why you are showing an interest for developing your public speaking skills, at this stage of your life, is because deep down within you there is a passion for something that you wish to present to the world, and only *you* know how to make it happen.

Whether you realize it or not, you have come to a level of awareness in life that is about to make you the best *you*. A better job opportunity might have been what prompted you to face your fear of public speaking, but the possibility of achieving a better job is just the motivation you needed in order to prepare you for what you are about to awaken within your inner being. You are about to let your inner genie out of its bottle.

Speaking Potion will supply you with the confidence to rely on your personal passion, to achieve your desired public speaking goals. Whether it's to obtain the career of your dream or to effectively lead a team, *Speaking Potion* will provide you with the right tools for the job and place you ahead in the game. The best thing about all of this is that you are already embedded with the most necessary tools that you will need. Simple things that you use in your everyday life (that you sometimes overlook) are capable of making you a better public speaker. Once you understand how to use these things to your advantage as a public speaker, you will begin to master your craft.

Do you know that you can learn certain tricks of the trade by watching shows like *Saturday Night Live, Good Morning America, Live with Kelly and Ryan, The Talk, The View, The Real, Wendy,* and *TMZ*, as well as by listening to talk radio shows like *The Sean Hannity Show, The Rush Limbaugh Show, The Micheal Berry Show, Steve Harvey Morning Show, The Breakfast Club,* and *NPR*. As you watch or listen to these shows, learn to look out for the "connection signals." Connection signals are certain things that the hosts say or do that resonates with the audience. Usually, you will be able to point out these connection signals, especially during heartfelt moments. These are the times when you can't help but to recognize the humane side of the person you're watching or listening to.

When a host is talking from the heart, the audience members facial expressions and mannerisms will change. They will lean forward, become more attentive—a sign that they are emotionally invested in the story being told. This method is best used when you know how to recognize your audience. Depending on your subject of discussion, you can captivate every individual in the crowd while making them feel as if they can relate to you on a much more personal level than the TV or radio allows. You can take them out of their world and bring them into yours. Or the situation might call for you to step out of *your* world and step into theirs. That's a decision that you will have to make after you are able to properly analyze the situation.

The more experience you obtain as a public speaker, the easier that choice will be to make. It will become second nature. In order to get to that level of expertise, you must exercise with and utilize all of the tools of the basic dynamics of public speaking. As you go through each phase, your level of comfortability will become more natural. If you are prepared, you will always remember the simple steps to take to get through your introduction.

These steps are nothing more than heat used to melt the ice. Once the ice melted, you can hop on your surfboard and ride the waves. How do you know when you are riding the waves? When you are able to make your words glide elegantly through the air and into the ears of your peers/audience members. The most effective way to achieve this desired result is by speaking on topics that you are already familiar with (or, preferably, have mastered).

When you speak on a topic you are knowledgeable about, you can be in front of a crowd of a million people and feel as if you are speaking to a friend. My advice to you is to tap into your life experiences and find the moments that are the most memorable, then dissect them, analyze them, and find something valuable within them that can be shared with the world. Practice this, make it a habit. Whether it's your first kiss or a bad relationship that almost sunk your ship, find the lessons to be learned in them and share it with your audience. Find the humor in a horrible event that you experience. Share it with your audience as you laugh at yourself. You'll be amazed at how much easier, and quicker, people will gravitate towards you when you are being your true self.

You might even want to look at it like you're at a therapy session with a crowd of therapists. Use a natural conversational approach to just talk to your audience. They're listening. Greet them with love, respect, and enthusiasm. Tell them why you are the most credible person to speak on this subject. Emphasize the two most important points of your speech, say something profound that will grab their attention, and force them to give you their undivided attention. Talk to them.

Make them understand why what you are saying is so important in their lives. Maintain eye contact with everyone as you speak. Wow them with simplicity. Make each person feel as if he or she is the only person in the room with you. If you are in a big enough room or stage, walk across it to cover every angle while interacting with the audience. Feel their energy. Use gestures when necessary—and as much as possible—to get your point across. Never give the audience your back. Someone might feel disrespected, and in return make it their business to sabotage your presentation.

Get the crowd to participate as much as possible by asking them questions and carefully listening to their answers. Make them feel as if they are on the stage with you. If someone in the audience says something funny, or if you happen to say something funny that made the whole crowd laugh, turn it into a repeating phrase. Smile at the audience every time you repeat it. When you get to a point where you can't seem to remember your next line, word, sentence, or phrase, pause. Then, come back with a question so that it will seem as if you paused for the benefit of the crowd.

Make sure you are always watching the audience, scanning it for signs of when to do what and for how long. Certain people's body language will help you determine the effectiveness of your message. But no matter what, focus on your message. Don't allow yourself to be sidetracked by anyone in the audience. You have to display a confident demeanor in order to be taken seriously. If the audience sees any signs of nervousness in you, they will lose interest in listening to what you are saying. Understand that you are dealing with people that are no different than yourself. Some of the same things that make you tick can make them tick. The same things that get you excited can get them excited. Incite excitement.

Use voice inflection to modify the tone of your speech when necessary. Pull your audience in right from the start, word by word, sentence by sentence, paragraph by paragraph. Be assertive in your pronunciation of every syllable. Be coherent as you radiate with self-confidence. When you come upon certain words that are powerfully effective, place emphasis on them by changing your pitch: shout, yell, scream. Speed up or slow down your pace. Drop your voice.

It is essential that you find a way to connect with your audience because it can mean the difference between you eating or going hungry, having a roof over your head, or being homeless. As crazy as this might sound, you may want to look at an audience as if everyone is a dollar sign. In reality that will most likely be the case. Wherever there's a large gathering, someone's profiting. Whether the venue is a hotel, ballroom, gymnasium, or stadium, people—from the vendors to the ticket sellers—are profiting. If you're there as a speaker, it's only right that you get a piece of the public speaking pie. The best way to guarantee that you do is to always stay sharp. Practice, practice, practice—and when you're done practicing, practice again.

Take advantage of every speaking opportunity you get, even if it's just idle conversation with a friend. Sharpen your sword. Keep yourself in great shape physically, mentally, and emotionally. When you feel good, you look good. When you look and feel good, you give off good energy. In return, good things happen in your life.

Public speaking skills are easy to acquire. Why? Because naturally the ability to communicate has been embedded in you since birth. As an adult, you've had years of experience practicing your oratory skills. Your lack of self-confidence as a public speaker has nothing to do with actually speaking. This hindrance comes from you being unprepared and unconnected to your topic. That is why when you practice promoting your passion, your positive qualities will help you deliver a polished speech as long as you speak from the heart. Simplify your message by using easy-to-understand words. You will fluently and effortlessly deliver your content in a sensible way that will get your message across to everyone listening.

Jen: "You mean like how you are effortlessly getting your message across to me right now?"

Joe: "Exactly. But if you really want to experience the full effect of *Speaking Potion*, come by and I'll explain it all to you much better in person. What do you say'?"

Jen: "No thanks. I think I'll pass on that for now. We can use the time it will take for me to get to you to read some more chapters over the phone."

Joe: "Okay, if you insist. I just wanted to add some visual to the audio to make it easier for you to grasp."

Jen: "You sure that's the only reason why you want me to come by your place, Joe? I highly doubt it."

Joe: "Okay, you got me. What can I say, Jen, you know me so well. I couldn't pull one over on you, not even in your sleep."

Jen: "Speaking of sleeping, I haven't been able to get much of that done lately."

Joe: "Why not? Are you staying up all night thinking about *him*?"

Jen: "No. I kinda got over the Jason situation."

Joe: "Good. That guy was no good for you anyway. A man that would cheat on a woman as beautiful and smart as you is insane and deserves to be locked up in an asylum with a straightjacket wrapped up around his entire body."

Jen: "Thanks, Joe."

Joe: "For what?"

Jen: "For saying that I'm smart."

Joe: "And don't forget the beautiful part! But, Jen, seriously, do you understand everything I read to you from chapter one?

Jen: "That was a lot of stuff, but I think I got it. I mean, I understand. I'd never looked at public speaking as an instrument of justice."

Joe: "I'm glad that you are able to see it that way. It shows you have a greater understanding than most people who've used the skills for their own self-interest."

Jen: "Well, it's really not me Joe, its you. The way you've just explained things to me made me realize that it's not just about me. I have to give in order to get. What I give of myself I get back: honesty, trust, and the opportunity to receive the love of my peers."

Joe: "And from your understanding, what was the most important lesson you learned from chapter one?"

Jen: "I learned that as long as I speak from the heart, and if possible find a way to simplify my message, people will listen to me. But I have to speak about things that affect me deeply, or things that affect people who are not able to speak for themselves."

Joe: "Great! So I guess you understand what you need to do now then, huh?"

Jen: "I definitely understand what I need to do. Thank you, Joe, you've been real helpful. As usual."

Joe: "So you think that's it, huh? You think understanding is all that there is to public speaking? Jen, go turn on your TV and your radio, too."

Jen: "For what Joe?"

Joe: "For chapter two: watch, listen, and learn."

Jen: "Okay, lets get started. I'm all ears."

· CHAPTER 2 ·

WATCH, LISTEN, & LEARN

Watch, listen, and learn from public speakers as they interact with their audience. You don't even have to leave your home to do this. The television can be a great teacher once you understand what it is that you are looking *for* instead of *at*. Looking *for* and looking *at* are synonymous to assets and liabilities. Next time you watch TV, train your eyes to look for the signs of a great public speaker. It doesn't matter what you are watching. You will always come across an individual that you will be able to pick up something from.

There are many tricks to the art of public speaking. When you are a beginner, you have to watch, listen, and learn so that you can know what styles and techniques will be best for you to borrow from and add to your own arsenal. For example, if you are someone that likes to watch the news, the reporters who are standing can teach you more than the ones sitting. Sitters are usually great with facial expressions and oratory skills, but you will need to learn much more.

It's the newscasters that are standing, moving around, and interacting with the audience/camera. You will learn the most from them. You can learn the different styles of body movements, especially the movements of the hands. As you begin to delve deeper into the public speaking realm, you will start to notice the different ways that a person's hands show whether you are dealing with a professional or an amateur. In cultures where speaking with your hands is natural, they have an advantage over those of us that were brought up in a culture where it is considered disrespectful. To some people, they might interpret it as an act of aggression or being uneducated.

Being able to master the movements of your hands is necessary. When you are giving a speech, with or without a podium, you will need to get a little animated in order to keep your crowd's attention. People get bored easily when forced to only use one of their five senses. If you can get them to use at least two, you'll have a better chance of keeping their attention longer. As they are watching you with their eyes, don't be a star that stands still. Be the cloud. Move around while shifting shapes in front of their eyes. Make them wonder what you're going to do next. Are you going to flap your arms like a bird while telling them the sky is the limit? Or are you going to hug yourself while slightly shivering to emphasize feeling frigid? Gesturing is a form of non-verbal speech.

If you were trying to communicate to a crowd the importance of ridding the neighborhood of a foul odor, would you say it verbatim, or would you hold your nose in disgust as you mentioned the words? Now, saying it verbatim without implementing any gestures might get you your desired result, but when you use the gesture it adds an extra sense of urgency to your cause. It gives your words impact, credibility. Most importantly, it brings to life the smell in the mind of your audience. Without ever having to smell it themselves. every time they think about it the picture of you holding onto your nose will appear in their mind. You've just left a lasting impression by using that one simple gesture. The third gesture you can use is what I call the "golden touch." If you can learn to master the golden touch, you will have the crowd eating from the palm of your hands.

The golden touch requires using creativity. People are always grateful for a speaker that can make them laugh, smile, and think. In most conversation or speech, there will always be objects of discussion that are not momentarily at your convenience, unless you are equipped with props. So this is when you use your imagination and tap into your creative power. If you are talking about a baseball bat, you can place your body into a stance as if you are about to take a swing at a ball, form your hands around an imaginary stick (like you're holding onto the bat), and swing it at the air. Homerun! You just got your point across by using that one simple gesture.

You can learn a lot of public speaking techniques on your free time in the comfort of your own home. Turn your television into a tunnel vision. Watch only the channels/programs that will help you progress at being a public speaker. Expose your mind to all forms of public speaking. You can learn how to paint vivid images in your listeners minds through storytelling—especially stories with moral endings that can help you to transition into your message.

For example, you may not be religious, but you can learn a lot watching professionals like Billy Graham, Joel Olsteen, Joyce Myers, and T.D. Jakes. These religious leaders have audiences by the hundreds of thousands. Watch them as they interact with their audience. Listen to how they speak. Do you hear the passion in their voice? Learn how to do what they do so that one day you, too, can have the courage, confidence, and coherency to speak to a super-size crowd. Turn your TV into your tutor. Learn some floor dynamics by watching meteorologists like Amie Freeze and newscasters like Rosanna Scotto. You can even learn while watching the Home Shopping Network. Some of the best public speakers are right there on your screen trying to sell you big screen TVs, pants, sweaters, shirts, leggings, wedding dresses, or George Foreman grills.

Even daytime TV shows like *The View, The Real, Ellen, Rachel Ray, Maury,* and *Jerry Springer* can all be used as a learning tool. Dedicate yourself to mastering the art of public speaking. In your spare time, log on to YouTube and watch some tutorials on public speaking. Watch, listen, and learn from the professional public speakers. Use everything in your surroundings, environment, and life to teach yourself.

Whenever you are in a group of people, absorb into the background and watch to see who the majority of the people gravitate towards. Ask yourself: Why do people gravitate to this individual? Then, answer your own question by watching that person. Take a few minutes to become aware. Consciously study them. Do they have any qualities that you may lack? Do they have any distinctive features? How does the way they use their voice contribute to gaining the attention of the crowd? Are they aggressive, passive, neither, or both? Watch their body movements. Are they animated? If so, to what extent? Which parts of the body do they use the most to interact? Do they equally divide their attention among the members of the group, or only focus on a few people? Do they give constant eye contact? Do they smile a lot, little, or not at all? Is everyone present fully engaged? What makes the topic of discussion so interesting to everyone? Is humor being used? If so, how often? Are there stories being told? If so, are the stories funny, educational, emotional, personal, moral, or motivational? Do they give the audience a chance to ask any questions? When and if an audience member speaks, how long do they usually hold the floor for before they take back command? What do you like most about their style?

As you watch people around you interact with one another, be aware of what's happening. Every day of your life you are presented with opportunities to watch the actions of public speakers, listen to the words of public speakers, and learn from fellow public speakers. Don't be closed-minded enough to think that you won't learn anything from the person working at your local supermarket, the attendant at the gas station, or any other person whose job requires them to communicate with the public on a daily basis. These people are also public speakers. Part of their profession is to effectively get their message across, sometimes to groups of people, depending on the situation.

When the check out line gets too backed up and the customers are becoming impatient, it is the job of the cashier to speak to all of the customers coherently and in a courteous manner and tone that helps alleviate the problem. Same thing applies to a McDonald's worker or a gas station attendant. When the horns are blaring and cars are riding each other's tails, the worker will have to communicate with the drivers in a way that helps calm everything down and saves the business from losing any money or loyal customers. The same way some people make bird watching their hobby, you should want to make people watching one of your new hobbies. Observation is a method that scientists use when analyzing anything they wish to understand and conquer. You should want to do the same.

Through watching and listening, you will learn everything that you need to know in preparing you for the world of public speaking. As an individual, you naturally are embedded with all the ingredients that make up the speaking potion. You have the same abilities you see, and admire, in professional public speakers; however, yours are special and uniquely designed to cater to your audience.

That's right. *Your* audience. Everyone has an audience that's willing to listen to what you have to say, no matter what the message may be. There is an audience for every message, like there is a woman for every man. Whether your message is based on love, hate, life, death, poverty, wealth, heaven, or earth. Even if you were to somehow create a public speaking platform based on something that only *you* like and care about, sooner or later you would begin to accumulate a number of followers/listeners. Why? Because we are all connected. If your hobby is collecting ants, you may find millions of people around the world that share the same interest. No matter what it is you want, like, or want to share with the world, there will always be people to accept it/you.

That is one of the reasons why there are so many different websites on the internet catering to everything from foodies and groupies to loonies and old school black and white movies. Whatever it is that you are passionate about, you will always find like-minded people that you can speak to and help build your self-confidence. Do not allow your fears of speaking in public to become an obstacle that stagnates your growth. There is an ultimate purpose for you wanting to overcome your fear of public speaking. You were meant to use your voice to accomplish great things in life. You are meant to put your passion into action, and change the world into what you imagine. You are not alone in your mission. Remember, I was once just like you, and—to a certain extent—still am. I wrote *Speaking Potion* with a desire to connect spiritually and emotionally to the billions of dormant speakers with profound, world-changing messages and ideas, but who have not yet exercised their natural born ability to effectively communicate with the rest of the world.

I strongly believe we all have a message that must be shared with the rest of the world. It is our duty to be in tune with everything and everyone in our surrounding in order to properly transfer and receive the power of public speaking. Awareness plays a big part in all of this (and by awareness, I mean listening). Being able to listen to what's going on around you can make the difference between life and death, true love and deception, failure and success. You've probably heard the saying, "You have two ears so that you can listen twice as much as you speak!" Well, I believe that statement to be an absolute truth. Listening is the fuel that you will need in order to keep the motor of your mouth running. The more you listen, the more information you are able to retain. The more information you retain, the more effective of a speaker you will become. Being a good listener makes you a better speaker. Not only will you be able to remember the things that you hear, but you will also be able to repeat things. The average person who is not listening to the speaker will not have any advantages over you. That puts you ahead of the game now.

Listening is a sign of respect, maturity, and discipline. It shows that you are able to pay attention. You're interested in what the other person has to say. You're present, ready to take action. Being a good listener is critical to learning how to perfect your public speaking craft. Like a job that requires you to receive training before you can start, public speaking is no different. Learning to listen is a training session in harnessing your thoughts so that you can deliver the best speech possible. A good listener will always be ready with a proper response because he or she won't just react to a situation, they will carefully measure it.

A good listener is similar to an anthropologist. As a subject is speaking he or she will be analyzed. The person speaking can come to represent an onion because so many layers of the individual's character will be peeled off by the time they are done speaking. A good listener would have come to an understanding of who the speaker truly is, what message he or she is trying to get across, where the person comes from, and why it is important to be for or against this individual. Knowledge is obtained through listening.

In fact, you can learn more about someone by listening to them than by watching them. Why? Because looks can be deceiving. People can make you believe that they are someone that they're not, simply by looking the part. But, when it comes to talking the talk, you can detect a fraud with your eyes closed, blindfolded. All you have to do is listen as the person speaks. If you know what to listen for, you will be able to spot a fake from a word away. That's right: a word.

If I was to tell you that I am a manager at a music equipment store, it would be expected of me to know the names of most, if not all, musical instruments. If asked about a string instrument and I wasn't able to explain the difference between a bass and an acoustic guitar, that should raise a red flag of fraud. Or if I was asked about a Casio keyboard and I answered, "I'm sorry but Mr. Casio doesn't work at the store anymore. He retired and took all his keyboards with him. May I help you with something else perhaps?" You definitely know that I was lying about who I said I was because you listened closely enough to know the right questions to ask. Listening requires you to come out of yourself and step into the world of the person who is speaking. Depending on the distance between you and the speaker, listening can be a hard task.

Being a good observer and listener can require you to be able to read body movements, facial expressions, gestures, and switching in the pitch of ones tone. All these things are vital information that you will need to learn how to identify, and be able to use yourself when faced with the opportunity to deliver a speech. Make it a habit of yours every time you converse with someone to remember when they grabbed your attention. Was it in the beginning, middle, or end? What did they say to grab your attention and keep it? Can that same attention gainer be used in giving a speech in front of a large audience?

Do the same things whenever you listen to anyone give a speech. Listen to hear if they used an attention gainer, made a declarative statement, or used a scenario or a quote. If they used a quote, find out who the source of the quote is. That research can tell you a lot about the speaker. Most people quote famous men and women whom they respect, admire, and wish to be like. Your listening ears can transmit all the necessary information to your brain for you to dissect, interpret, and then come to your own conclusion on how best to deal with the matter at hand. This method can and should be used in all walks of life, from romantic relationships, business, friendships, family matters to every interaction that requires communication.

Some might say being a good listener requires you to have a good memory, but that's not always necessary. You can be just as effective with a pad and pen at hand. That's right, take notes. Taking notes while listening or watching, can help you to highlight major key points that you can later touch on. Most speakers will be delighted to know that you were interested enough about the topic to have taken notes. Taking notes is a sign of maturity, intellectualism, devotion, and passion.

Now, last but not least, learn everything that you can about public speaking. Everyday you wake up, make it your business to learn one new thing about public speaking. Have fun with your learning process. Be creative. Pick a new word from the dictionary every morning and use that word throughout the whole day with everyone you come in contact with. You can make the words random or go through the whole alphabet from A to Z. By the end of your first year, you will have learned 365 new words to add to your vocabulary. Your new learned vocabulary words can raise your value as a speaker.

Speaking of valuable speakers, you should get into the habit of listening to different radio hosts. You can learn a lot from some of the best radio personalities in the United States, especially radio hosts who speaks on politics. These people are very passionate about what they believe. When you listen to them, you get a sense of how it feels to stand for something that you do believe in with your heart, mind, body, and soul.

I would recommend that you start listening to these four extraordinary personalities: Rush Limbaugh, Micheal Berry, Sean Hannity, and Bill Cunningham. Becoming a great public speaker is a full-time job, but you also must have the passion for speaking in order to have fun with it. Right now, overcoming your fear of public speaking might be a challenge; however, it is a challenge that you should take on with the understanding that once you conquer this fear, you will be able to achieve anything you put your mind to. Just picture yourself in the position of the people you are learning from. Why? Well because there is a part of the brain that can materialize what it sees. I will expound on it more in the next chapter. Right now, you are in the learning phase. Absorb everything.

You have to understand that the world is one big school and we are all students. Even those of us that teach are still on the same path as those who are learning. The process of obtaining knowledge of the world and of self is a never-ending mission. We live in a very complex world, and we are very complex people. Navigating our way through the earth's many terrains requires one to become fully engaged with everything that is part of the environment. It's the same way you have to become fully engaged with everything related to public speaking.

Every day someone in the public is speaking up about something. All around you the environment is speaking to you. For this reason, we experience things like global warming, earthquakes, floodings, and a long list of other occurrences that we thought were natural. What is happening is that the world is trying to speak to us, and we need to start listening before it's too late. We need to learn from what we are watching. The earth is our home; it is the responsibility of each and every one of us to take care of it. In turn, it will take care of us. Everything we as humans need to survive is freely given to us by nature. *You* are a part of nature. If becoming a public speaker is what you need to survive, dig into your natural self. You will find everything you need to succeed. Watch yourself, listen to yourself, and learn from yourself.

When I say yourself, I don't mean just you—I mean everyone that breathes the same air as you, eats the same foods as you, because we are all in this together. Whether we choose to accept it or not.

Joe: "This, Jen, is why I advised you to study all those TV personalities, radio show hosts, and internet bloggers and podcasters."

Jen: "Wow Joe, I never knew you admired so many TV personalities."

Joe: "Not just TV personalities, Jen. Radio hosts, too."

Jen: "That's right. Radio hosts, too. Personally, I don't listen to too much public radio. Too many commercials for me. Although I do listen to Z100 and the Breakfast Club in the morning. Other than that it's usually commercial-free iHeartRadio."

Joe: "Hey, to each his own. Me, I don't mind the commercials. I listen to them, too. You want to know why?"

Jen: "Why Joe? Why? *Please* tell me why. And it better be good."

Joe: "Commercials are a source of information. They let you know what's in, what's out, what's coming, who's losing, who's winning. And some are even entertaining."

Jen: "Oh yeah, you mean like the Doritos commercial at the last Superbowl? Or the—"

Joe: "Hold that thought. Jen, if I asked you to tell me what you've learned from chapter two, 'Watch, Listen, & Learn,' what would you tell me?"

Jen: "Well, Joe, I would tell you that I've learned that I'm presented with opportunities every day to watch everything and everyone around me, including the television and the internet. Oh, and I can't forget about the radio. I have opportunities to listen to everyone and analyze the responses that people receive. from the things they say to the things they do. And by doing all of this, I will learn the things I need to know."

Joe: "Looks like you got it. Now it's time for us to move on to the next chapter: 'The Copycat Effect.'"

Jen: "Joe, wait! Let me turn off the TV and radio first.... Okay, I'm ready! Let's go."

· CHAPTER 3 ·

THE COPYCAT EFFECT

The copycat effect is one of the easiest ways to learn how to become what you desire. Children do it all the time, and they are the best at it. Once a child sets his or her mind on something in order for them to understand what it is they are dealing with, the child will adapt the character traits of the object and attempt to communicate with it as such. That's why sometimes you might catch a young boy or girl barking like a dog or meowing like a cat. They are using the copycat effect to navigate around their environment. You can use the same method. It will work for you much more effectively, due to the fact that you are operating with a fully developed brain.

Unconsciously, many of us use this method in our lives all the time—usually all for the wrong reasons, such as to recite the newest pop song on the radio, animatedly explain to a friend the details of a current event, or mimic the newest dance moves. If you were to place the same amount of energy into reciting a speech that *you* wrote, don't you know that you would get a much better result. The fact that it is something of your own creation-will make it that much easier for you to master it. Unless you believe the words of a stranger are more important to remember than your own, there is no reason why you shouldn't always put yourself first. You can use the copycat effect on yourself whenever you come across something about you that is intriguing or needs to be repeated until it becomes a habitual act or response.

Don't be afraid to make fun of yourself. Let your inner child out. Once upon a time all adults were children, so it won't be hard to find some adults that will relate to your childish antics. In fact, you might trigger some fun and memorable times in their lives that puts a smile on their face. The copycat effect is commonly used by comedians to get a laugh out of their audience.

Comics like Kevin Hart will use voice inflections to change his tone from an adult to that of a child or use vigorous gestures when talking about his kids and the hilarious things that they do. So, if you are a parent, turn the time you spend with your children into learning experiences. As a public speaker, you will come across times when you will have to deliver a speech in front of young kids or teenage audience. To get your message across effectively, it will be great if you can use certain mannerisms and terminologies that they are familiar with. This will help you to get and keep their attention. The copycat effect is a valuable tool to have in your possession because in whatever style of public speaking you lack the most, you can use the copycat effect to develop that weakness into a strength.

Do you lack charisma? If so the best way to build a charismatic persona is by simply being yourself. I know that might sound crazy, but just think about it. What is charisma? Well, according to the *American Heritage College Dictionary, Third Edition*, charisma is a) rare personal quality of leaders who arouse fervent popular devotion and enthusiasm; b) personal magnetism or charm. Now, the reason I believe that you can be charismatic by being yourself is because charisma is all about the "personal" (i.e., person).

Each person living has that personal magnetism in them. By reading *Speaking Potion*, it proves that you are devoted and enthusiastic about becoming a great public speaker. If you weren't, you would not be reading this right now. You would be doing what everyone else is doing. Being that you're not, that means you are a leader. The personal magnetism and charm that comes with being charismatic is already naturally embedded in you. You will need to realize that your passion is your purpose in order to present your charisma to the world. Once you come to this profound realization, you will obtain the power and ability to work miracles.

A lot of people don't believe how easy life can become for them. Instead of taking the smooth, straight road, they veer onto the crooked, bumpy, fast-paced highway of life, and end up either crashing into each other or trying to get off at the wrong exit. Never go against yourself. It is unnatural for you to willingly continue playing a game that was rigged for you to lose. Why choose to lose in life when you are truly a natural born winner?

We all have a map within us. Some choose to call it the "moral compass" that directs us on the path to our every destination. Allow the leader within you to lead you, and your outcomes will always be successful. You can use the copycat effect to lock onto certain characteristics of you that are important for having in your possession for your journey. The human mind is like a computer: the more information you download into your database, the more useful you are to the world and the much better your chances at succeeding becomes. Although I said that it's good to take and borrow from others in order to grow and build yourself, it doesn't have to be in the literal sense.

Learning from someone else's mistakes is a form of taking and borrowing from them. Imagine you are attending a function where there is a speaker giving a speech on the importance of having a diverse workplace. While you are using the restroom, you overhear someone say, "Hey, Dave make sure you get rid of all the applicants with muslim names. We don't need to have them in our company." Now, as you are washing your hands, the speaker comes out of the stall where you overheard the person giving an order to discriminate. What's one lesson you could learn from the speaker's mistake?

As a novice in the public speaking field, the copycat effect is best used for collecting and storing positive qualities that you can later put into effect as you become more affluent at speaking in front of a crowd. Naturally, your charisma will exude because you will gain the confidence to properly present your passion without it being unconsciously tainted by the negative influence of others. It becomes easier for you to be your natural genuine self. Through learning from the experiences and mistakes of an insurmountable number of people who came before us. We now know the results, the outcomes of those who choose to go against their natural self. Nature will always triumph. The natural will always win.

Anything that you may feel you lack in life, you will see it in others and be able to find it within yourself. The problem with some of us is that we look to how the rest of the world chooses to define certain things as the truth and finality. Well, it might be for those who've accepted it as such. As an individual, you should always want to define *you* from your own perspective. *That* is the key to your charisma—or, as some will like to call it, swag.

Having charisma is nothing more than being who you are with a sense of confidence that shows you fully accept who you are. There is no one set way of being charismatic. Charisma can be displayed by anyone. From some of the most feared and hated people of the world to some of the most respected and loved. Evil men like Adolf Hitler, Jim Jones, and countless others were all said to have charisma while great men and women like Martin Luther King Jr., Abraham Lincoln, Mother Teresa, Madam C.J. Walker, and more were also said to have charisma.

So, don't ever doubt yourself into believing that you lack *anything*. And if you do, simply use the copycat effect on yourself. Like a farmer would plant seeds in order to reap the fruits of his labor, plant seeds of charisma in your mental garden. Cultivate it through conversations with like-minded individuals. The more people you converse and associate with, the easier it will become for you to showcase your charismatic ways. Be aware of how people react to you when you converse with them. Watch their facial expressions to see if they smile a lot. A person smiling is almost always a sign of the power of charisma at work.

As a matter of fact, start getting into the habit of keeping a smile on your own face as you speak. People who are "smiling speakers" come off as being naturally charismatic. Practice this by spending at least five to ten minutes per day looking at yourself in the mirror as you speak to your reflection. Find the facial expressions that best represent who you are and what you stand for. Find the facial expressions you think are the most charismatic and practice using them on your family and friends before introducing them to strangers. Master your most favorite charismatic expressions, then practice using other people's facial expressions.

The reason I'm suggesting you practice learning other people's facial expressions is so that you can build a library of copycat expressions. All of the different expressions in your mental library will come in handy when dealing with different groups of people from varying geographic locations and backgrounds. Learn to familiarize yourself with certain mannerisms of different ethnic groups. Learn certain terminologies that are currently popular. That way when you use the copycat effect with them, it will be genuine and not look like you are just trying to appease to this particular group of people for your own self-interest.

If you'd kept up with the 2012 election campaign, you remember the presidential candidate, Hillary Clinton, was speaking in an African American church in the South. She said something along the line of, "...Nobody said it was going to be easy." Most blacks cringed at the sound of her voice saying those words. It wasn't because of what she said but how she said it. Mrs. Clinton had used the copycat effect to inflect her voice to make herself sound as if she was an African American woman from the South.

Conservative talk show radio hosts like Micheal Berry, Mark Levine, Rush Limbaugh, and Sean Hannity had a field day playing the recording over and over to their audience in order to discredit her as someone who will say and do *anything* to solidify the votes. I believe had Mrs. Clinton stayed true to herself and her message, she would have had a better chance at winning more supporters. As a public speaker, you will always be scrutinized and analyzed. Anything wrong that comes out of your mouth can be made to jeopardize you. The copycat effect can backfire if not used right, as in the case with Mrs. Clinton (and I'm sure many others).

The copycat effect is a tool that can be used for good or evil. Your motive for using it should always be to do good things that can benefit others more than to benefit yourself. Your career as a public speaker, or public figure, can blow up in your face before it even gets started. Have you ever seen the show *Catfish* on MTV? This show is the perfect example of what can happen when people use the copycat effect for all the wrong reasons. The show *Catfish* is based around people who use photos of friends, family members, and/or strangers to build profiles on social media, which they use to attract other people who they feel wouldn't normally be attracted to them. Sometimes emotions get involved and long-lasting relationships are built on the basis of texting and conversing over the phone and internet.

Like the law of gravity, what goes up must come down. Anytime you build anything off lies, it will one day be destroyed by the truth. Everything in darkness will one day come to light. So, you can imagine all the disappointment and heartache that goes down while the show goes on. As the producers of the show continue to profit from all of these acts of illusion, the faux who used the copycat effect for fraudulent reasons are now known by everyone all over the world that watch the show as liars, deceivers, and people that should not be trusted.

Ones reputation can get ruined pretty quickly after committing such a deceitful act. It might become hard for you to get a job, make new friends, and/or ever get involved in a serious, intimate relationship. This is why I believe it is important for you to know yourself, love yourself, and be yourself. The more comfortable you are with who you are, the less likely you are to ever try to present yourself as someone else. You must accept yourself before others can accept you. Using the copycat effect properly will help you do just that.

I would like to share a quick little story with you on how using the copycat effect helped a young neighbor of mine win some money at a talent show. Michelle was a seven-year-old girl who'd just moved into the neighborhood with her father, Mike, who worked as a police officer. On my way home from work one day, I came upon Michelle crying as she sat on the stoop in front of her house. Normally I would mind my own business and just go in the house to take a nap, but hearing little Michelle's cries stopped me in my tracks just when I was about to place my keys in the door.

I turned around and walked over to her house, which was right next door to mine. I looked down at little Michelle with sympathy in my face, and I asked her, "Hey, Michelle, what's the matter little lady?" Michelle continued to cry and kept her head down on her lap. I thought maybe she didn't hear me. So, I asked again, but this time I raised my voice a little bit louder. "Michelle, what's the matter are you okay?"

Sniffling, Michelle looked up at me with sadness in her face, wiped the tears from under her eyes and said, "Hi, Mr. Johnson. Sorry about the tears and the noise."

I smiled at her and consoled her. "It's okay, Michelle, even I cry sometimes. What's the matter? Is everything alright?" I inquired.

She sniffled. "No. My daddy's birthday is coming up, and I want to buy him a nice tie to wear with his suit and I don't have enough money," she sobbed.

Feeling sorry for Michelle, I went into my pocket, pulled out my wallet, and asked, "How much do you need?"

Michelle pushed my hand away and said, "No thanks, Mr. Jay. My dad told me nothing in life is free, and that anything I want I have to work for. So I can't accept your money."

I was floored by her response, and at the same time admired her for her tenacity. "Okay," I said. "Well if you don't want me to give you the money, I don't know what else I can do."

Michelle sighed and shared, "There's a talent show competition at my school, and the winning prize is $100. Just enough to buy the tie."

"Great!" I excitedly exclaimed, "You can join the competition and win the money to buy your dad the tie."

"I know, that's what I was thinking of doing, Mr. Jay, but I don't have a talent."

"Well can you sing?"

"No," she responded defeatedly.

"Can you dance?"

"No." She crossed her arms over her chest.

I thought about her situation for a second, and then it came to me: the copycat effect. "Wait right here for a second, Michelle." I then ran into the basement of my house and brought back my collection of music and dance DVDs and handed them over to Michelle.

"What's that for, Mr. Johnson? You want me to have a yard sale?"

I laughed, "No, Michelle. But what you can do is play these DVDs, watch how they dance, and try to do what they do. Listen to the music and try to sing how they sing."

She took the DVDs and said, "Well, I guess I can give it a try. I have three weeks before the talent show. Thank you, Mr. Jay." Michelle then sat up, hugged my leg, and then went into her home.

Joe: "But I'll tell you the end of that story later. Right now, I really need to know what have you learned from chapter three. What do you think about it, Jen? You know how much I value your opinion on things. So, give it to me straight."

Jen: "I think you should have named this chapter 'Monkey See, Monkey Do.' I love monkeys. Not that I have anything against cats, I just think monkeys are cuter, smarter, and more fun. If I ever become a rich girl, I'm going to build a zoo in my backyard and have lots of monkeys and—"

Joe: "Jen."

Jen: "Lions, tigers, and—"

Joe: "Jen!"

Jen: "Some therapy snakes and a bunch of—"

Joe: "Jen!!!! Before you continue on building your zoo, I have one very important question to ask you."

Jen: "Go ahead Joe, shoot."

Joe: "Were you listening when I went through chapter three with you, and if so, what have you learned?"

Jen: "First of all, Joe, I always listen when you speak, and what I've learned is that by mimicking myself and others I can build a storage house of different mannerisms and characters that can later be used as part of my presentations during speeches. I can create a sense of charisma, humor, and professionalism through the correct usage of the copycat effect. So there you have it. Now do you believe—"

Joe: "That you're ready to move on to chapter four? Yes, I do believe that you're ready to go out there and show the world that you're an eloquent speaker. I do believe you got it in you to be the best public speaker that the world has ever heard. I do believe you're ready to *talk your talk*."

Jen: "Talk my talk! Whatchu talkin' 'bout, Willis?"

Joe: "Give me a second to get a drink of water, and I'll tell you all about it.... Okay, you ready? Now lets go."

· CHAPTER 4 ·

TALK YOUR TALK

'Talk Your Talk' is my way of telling you to speak your truth. We are all born with a truth within us that the rest of the world needs to hear. Ever hear the saying, "The truth shall set you free?" Well, when applied to public speaking, this translates to "talk your talk." By using your heart to speak your mind, I believe an amateur can be perceived as a novice. This is when passion takes power and prevails over passiveness. When a person speaks from the heart, no matter what it is they are speaking about, people tend to listen. All of your public speaking weaknesses becomes non-existent.

If you are one of those people that starts to sweat, stutter, or shut down when you talk in front of a crowd, that is most likely because the subject that you are speaking on is not *your* truth. Before you can stand in front of a crowd of people for hours and speak on different subject matters, you must first learn how to stand on your own in front of a crowd and speak your truth.

Doing this will help mold you into becoming a better public speaker. When you are speaking on a subject that you are passionate about, you tend to be more relaxed, more versed, more knowledgeable, and more natural. The more personal the topic is to you, the easier it will be for you to deliver your message without having to resort to looking at a paper or teleprompter. If the words are from your heart, you will not need a speech writer because it is already written in your DNA. We are all born with a message inside of us.

Talking your talk is something that every one is able to do, but some of us would rather talk *a* talk. In the process of trying to talk *a* talk, we lose our natural abilities and our self-confidence. Once you allow the world or society to tell you who you are, you automatically adapt and accept everything that comes with the definition of your given label or persona. This is why it took me forty years to come to the understanding of who I'm not. Hopefully it won't take *you* as long to find yourself or your voice. You can cut your journey short right now and head directly to the source of who you are by beginning to talk your talk. Speak your truth.

If you grew up in a broken home where your father was an abusive alcoholic who treated your mother like his personal punching bag every time he got some liquor in his system, talk about it. Share your story with the world. Release all that suppressed energy into the universe and let it find new homes. Allow your story to help heal men and women that are struggling with alcohol addiction. Go to an AA meeting and share your experience as a child of someone that was addicted to drugs and/or alcohol. Tell those that are now struggling with the addiction about the effect it had on you growing up. Speak up about it, talk your talk. Speak from your heart and watch how effortlessly the right words begin to formulate into powerful sentences that will connect with the hearts of everyone and touch them emotionally. If you grew up in a stress-free, no-problems type of home, talk about it. Use your experience to motivate new couples on how to be good parents. If you grew up watching cartoons and reading a lot of comic books, you can probably tap into your memory bank to find a plethora of interesting information to talk about.

You will probably be able to give a seminar at a comic book convention or create a website filled with webinars and tutorials sharing your knowledge with people all across the world. We all have something that we can talk intelligently about. Whether it's something that we've personally experienced or something that someone else had experienced, it effected us. No matter how you look at it, it is your truth. Anything that touches you emotionally becomes part of your truth. It was powerful enough to invoke feelings within you that would have normally been suppressed.

To develop your public speaking skills using the "talk your talk" method, ask yourself these three questions: What do I love in this world more than anything? What do I hate in this world more than anything? What am I the most passionate about? Then time yourself with a stopwatch as you answer each question. See which question you spend the most time answering. Which ever one you had the most to speak on, *that* is most likely where your speaking strength is. Focus on writing some mini speeches on that topic. Get yourself more familiar with the subject. Look at it as a training session, harnessing your thoughts and finding your voice. This can help you to learn how to extend your speeches.

For example, if what you love the most in the world is to spend time with friends and family, you will probably want to talk about all the fun you have with each and every one separately before you speak about the whole group. Speaking about your parents may take twenty minutes or more, depending on their age and lifestyles. Your talk on them might be based on memories of you as their child and the things they had to do, as parents, to put up with you.

Talking about your siblings might take another twenty minutes, depending on whether they are younger or older than you are. Stories of childhood rivalries can extend the time, and should be used whenever possible to get a laugh out of your audience. When you get to talking about your nieces and nephews, that might take forty minutes (since children are always the most animated and entertaining). Your last twenty minutes you might want to spend it on talking about a couple of your closest friends. Now that was a fun and easy way to spend an hour, speaking about the people that you know and love.

Would you be able to spend the same amount of time speaking on what you hate most in the world more than anything? What about speaking on what you are the most passionate about? You need to know so that you can identify where your strength is. When you know where your strength is, it is easier for you to be an effective speaker and make people hear you when you talk. As you advance in the public speaking world, you never know how big of an audience you will attract. If you are going to be giving a lecture or speech in front of thousands of people, you should make it meaningful, real, heartfelt, passionate. Say something that's going to help change the world for the better.

Invoke the individual imagination of each member of the audience whenever possible. You can achieve that by using scenarios and allowing them to place themselves in the center of it all. Make them feel as if you are speaking their truth. As human beings, we've all been through, heard of, or seen some of the most bizarre things there are to experience. Everyone loves a good story. Talk about the things that effected you the most. Storytelling is a fun way to connect with your audience while simultaneously making them relate to your message.

As far as life experiences go, there's really nothing new under the sun. That means you will always find more than enough people that relate to whatever it is you are talking about. If you can figure out a way to incorporate a story or two here and there as you talk your talk, your audience will pay attention. Plus, the more you talk, the more comfortable you will become with yourself as your truth begins to speak through your jaw like sweat seeping through your pores. There is no reason for you to run out of things to speak about when you are talking your talk.

Your mind is a vault filled with valuable information about your life that is ready to be shared with the world. The best thing is that you're not being forced to speak. You're in control of the situation. Anything you don't feel comfortable sharing with others, you can keep to yourself. Depending on the crowd, sometimes it might be more favorable for you to divulge some personal information about yourself. That's what makes your audience trust you. That's what makes them want to hear more. The fact that you are being real with them is a rarity that they will greatly appreciate.

So many people nowadays do everything they can to become anything other than themselves. It is a relief to come across people who aren't afraid to show and tell you who they are. Whether it's their good, bad, or ugly side, they put it all out there on the table and leave it out for your interpretation. Imagine if all politicians were that honest about whom they truly are and what their true intentions are. There would be less corruption, deception, and problems in the world. Things would get done much faster because the right men and women for the job would always be on the job, getting done what the people put them in office to do.

Maybe you are someone with a passion for helping others. As a public speaker, you can be the conduit through which vital information and necessary resources spreads in struggling communities. Speaking for the well-being of others and helping the disadvantaged are honorable jobs that are available all across the United States, especially for bilingual individuals. If you are someone that speaks a second language, you can secure a second source of income in your spare time.

The many opportunities that come with being a public speaker are all yours to take advantage of. The reason a lot of these jobs are open is because most people are too scared to do exactly what you are doing right now: taking initiative. You may have a fear of public speaking, but by taking the initiative to purchase and read *Speaking Potion*, you've just placed yourself ahead of millions (if not billions) of people across the world who are choosing to do nothing about their fear of public speaking. Communicating with others is instrumental to our survival. The more people you can communicate with, the more valuable you'll become.

You can even create your own job opportunities based around the things that you know and are able to fluently talk about. Like I said before, there is nothing new under the sun. If you attended Catholic school your whole life and graduated with honors, you can now build a business around your very own experiences as a Catholic school student. All you would have to do is talk your talk. There are parents out there that would pay to learn how to keep their kids on the right path from kindergarten to high school graduation. If you are a success story in whichever field in life you are the most experienced, do the world a favor. Talk your talk.

Most motivational speakers are people who do just that. They talk their talk to people that understand where they are coming from. People who want to get to where they are in life. I believe everyone is skilled at something, either by nature or nurture. The environment you were raised in equipped you with certain skills that are valuable. Not only to others from that same environment, but especially to those who have no idea about how to survive that environment without first being formally trained, instructed, introduced, or initiated.

Your individual experience in life gives you the authority to speak on it exclusively from your point of view. The combined experiences of your life forms the vocabulary that allows you to talk your talk with authenticity. Every word that comes out of your mouth originated from your heart. So when you speak your mind, your whole body reacts in symphony with your thoughts. If what's in your heart isn't pure, then your thoughts will be off balance. When you attempt to communicate with your audience, they will be able to see right through you. Your own body will turn against you, and send out different signals to the audience, letting them know that you are not being true to yourself.

If you've ever witnessed a speaker who couldn't stop saying "umm" or "ahhh," took a lot of long pauses, avoided eye contact with the audience, avoided a question and answer session, or tried to use too much humor instead of focusing on getting the message across, that is usually because the speaker is misleading or deceiving the audience and is unprepared. Unless the speaker is a professional liar or is able to quickly and effectively recover from his mistakes, he will lose his audience. They will stop paying attention to what he is saying and start to speak amongst themselves. As a public speaker, this type of reaction can ruin your career.

This is why it's so important for you to talk your talk. When you fill your heart with impurities that don't coincide with what's in the rest of your body, it won't properly filter through your mind. There is power in speaking from the heart, keeping it real, being yourself. The most confident you can ever be in life is when you are being your true self. You might feel like your voice is too squeaky, too baritone, too low, or too loud. If that's who you are, *own it*. Don't try to change it in order to be accepted because when you do, you give away your power. Don't ever take away from your natural authentic self. You connect best with others when you are being *you*.

You can flourish as a speaker by appealing to peoples basic need to connect. The need to communicate with other human beings is as important as the need for food, clothing, and shelter. We are social creatures that need to be in the presence of other humans in order to *feel*. Without the ability to *feel*, we are no different from the lower animals. When you talk your talk and are able to make someone in your audience laugh, cry, smile, or want to be the last person to leave the venue so that they can shake your hands and congratulate you, there is no better feeling in the world.

With the use of technology, you can take your speech worldwide and make a touching delivery on Twitter, hand out verbal food on YouTube, promote your plans on Instagram, or just stay connected with folks on Facebook. Whether you know it or not, *you* have what it takes to be one of the greatest public speakers. We all do. Only difference between you and someone who is getting paid millions of dollars to speak in public is: they are doing it and you are learning about it. Therefore, your next step is to perfect the craft so that when you are presented with the opportunity, you can just do it.

Speaking about yourself, your life experiences, obstacles, goals, and dreams will come easy once you know what you want to share and what you don't. The second thing you will have to do is compartmentalize your stories so that you can retrieve the right one at the right time. If your aim is to get a laugh out of your audience, you should have a mental-shelf of humorous stories that you can choose from according to the type of audience you are speaking to. For whatever emotions you want to conjure from your audience, you should know where to go inside of yourself to get it.

Stay attuned with what's going on in the world around you. Sometimes you might see or hear something that someone else is going through that effects you so much, that you know without a doubt if anyone else was to see or hear, it would have the same effect on them.

Imagine you're sitting outside of a restaurant on a hot sunny day enjoying a slice of pizza. You happened to look across the street and see a homeless man with his wife and son digging through trash cans looking for their next meal. Now, out of nowhere, a young boy (holding a doggie bag) exiting the restaurant looks up at his mom and dad and points at the homeless family across the street. They then proceed to walk across the street together, and upon reaching the homeless family, the little boy gives his food to the homeless family, hugs them, holds onto their hands to say a prayer, and then walks away. Although you were just a witness to all of this, it is now part of your talk and you have the right to speak of it to anyone you wish. That story is something that you can store in your mental-shelf along with any other compassionate stories that you know.

Joe: "Aside from this story, Jen, what have you learned from my 'Talk Your Talk' lesson? What did you get out of the information?"

Jen: "OMG, Joe. I wish I knew all this information, like, when I was back in junior high or high school. It could have really helped me make friends with the right group of people."

Joe: "Jen, it's never too late in life to talk your talk. As a matter of fact, you're at the exact point in your life when talking your talk is going to matter the most. I mean, you did understand everything you were listening to, right?"

Jen: "Lets see... So, this is just me being me, talking my talk, speaking my truth. Letting people in on personal things about my life in order to bring their guards down and make connections, network."

Joe: "Yes, but why is it so important to talk your talk?"

Jen: "Well, it helps to create a bond between the audience and myself. The more people can relate to me, the more they will like me and want to hear me speak."

Joe: "I have to say, Jen, you're one smart cookie."

Jen: "Well, thanks. I just hope this cookie doesn't crumble when it's crunch time."

Joe: "What if I told you I can almost guarantee you that will never happen?"

Jen: "I would ask you how that is possible, and what do I have to do to make sure of it?"

Joe: "Simple. Be Yourself. Use your potion."

Jen: "Be myself! Use my potion! What are you talking about, Joe?"

Joe: "I'm talking about chapter five, 'Convert Your Passion.'"

Jen: "Sounds interesting. I'm listening. Talk to me, baby."

Joe: "Before I start, Jen, I want you to ask yourself: what is your number one goal in life? What's your purpose?"

· CHAPTER 5 ·

CONVERT YOUR PASSION

Connect with your pivoting passion professionally. This is an advice that I would suggest to everyone in the world that truly believes they know what their purpose in life is and are chasing their dreams daily by doing what's necessary no matter the sacrifice. Passion is the number one ingredient for the speaking potion.

Knowing what you are passionate about is the key element to living a happy life. When combined with proficiency, your passion can become your profession and in turn produce plentiful profit. I believe many people would quit their job and would rather work in a position where they are making less money doing something they love than to get paid more doing something they hate. After all, there's no better job than doing something you are passionate about.

Being disconnected from your life's passion can cause serious discomfort, disability, and despair. This can result in you having to lower your standards and settle for less than what you are worth. Many people wind up missing their calling and becoming complacent merely for the sake of survival. Unhappy marriages, disloyal spouses, debts, dead-end careers: these are some of the results from not following your life's passion. You settle for the mundane for the sake of security. Meanwhile, you are continually miserable.

Why would anyone wish to be a part of such a vicious cycle? Some people just don't know any better. Like the saying goes, "If you knew better, you'd do better." Well, I'm here to tell you that you *are* better. You were better before you began reading this book, and you will become *great* once you start applying the words of *Speaking Potion* into your life.

I want you to saturate your mind with each and every chapter of *Speaking Potion*. Let it all sink in and become part of your daily nutritional absorption. Fertilize your mind with these fresh ideas that are bound to help you blossom into a flourishing boss. Make your mark on the world by allowing your true self to show.

The world is full of unhappy people who've missed out on their purpose and destiny. They allowed others to define them instead of embracing who they are and displaying their own interests and qualities. It is easy to be who the rest of the world wants you to be. It takes courage and passion to be yourself, to stand firm on the things that you love and believe in. As a person on the journey to becoming a public speaker, one of the ways you can effortlessly develop great skills is by speaking on subjects you are passionate about. Let your passion be the potion that influences others to make you their spokesman. Your speaking skills can pay for your meals and bills.

You can achieve great success in life when you decide to exploit the natural talents that you are born with. Those gifts, I believe, were given to each and everyone of us as tools for cultivating an everlasting source of sustenance. Life is not meant to be hard, at least not for people that know who they are, where they came from, where they're going, how they're going to get there, and—most importantly—what they want out of life. All your choices should be based on that ultimate goal. All your actions should in one way or another coincide with achieving that goal. You will always reap what you sow.

As someone who wants or needs to master the art of public speaking, you should be planting "speech seeds." Not just any speech seeds—speech seeds that are connected to the things in life you are passionate about. So what are speech seeds? Well, I came up with the concept of speech seeds when I was going through my own struggles with overcoming my fear of public speaking.

I wrote five different speeches that were based on topics I'm passionate about, topics that moved me emotionally and made me want to take action. Each speech is a seed because the more I would practice reading the speech for memorization, the more confidence I'd grow. The more confident I became, the easier it got for me to recite each speech with fluency. My first planted speech seed was a speech on bullyism (a problem that is currently responsible for the deaths of many children across the nation).

As a father, bullying is a topic that I personally feel some emotional investment to because I don't have custody of my child. I'm not with him at all times to protect him, and I know how cruel kids can be to each other when unattended by adults. So, I wrote a speech that touched on the effects of bullyism while giving a solution to the problem. I believe bullyism is a form of hate. Like all other forms of hate, the only logical cure is love.

My first seed sowed was a seed of love. I wanted to put that energy out into the universe. Make it connect to as many people as possible so that, hopefully, it will help minimize the occurrence of young men and women committing suicide from being bullied.

Reciting that speech helped me tremendously, and motivated me to sow my second speech seed, which is a speech on ending the drug epidemic. I called my second speech seed "New War On Drugs." In it I speak on the crack cocaine and opioid epidemic, as well as the importance of using education and vocation as a tool to combat the drug epidemic instead of incarceration. In my speech, I argued for educating young men and women on the devastating effects of using and selling drugs and for creating vocational opportunities that will equip them with marketable skills for well-paying jobs. Through this, their desire to sell and use drugs will begin to diminish.

Those are two examples of how to plant speech seeds to help you grow as a public speaker. Ask yourself what you are passionate about. How can you use that passionate energy to help in the development as a public speaker? Easy. Write about it. Write everything that comes to your mind when you begin to think about what it is that gets you angry or makes you happy. Is it your job, hobby, or something that others do and you have absolutely no control over?

Whatever it is, write it out. Start with a word, a sentence, and then a paragraph. Find some place private where you can be alone and read it over to yourself in your head. Then, read it aloud. As you began to get more familiar with the topic, write some more. Get at least one page worth of writing on paper, then stop. Now take some more time to yourself to read everything you've written. Read it over and over again until you can memorize it. Once you have it all memorized, find a friend or family member and give them the paper to hold onto and read as you recite aloud what you've written down. Tell them to stop you every time you make a mistake.

I'd learned a lot from doing these exercises on a weekly basis. After going through my first speech on bullyism, doing the others became a fun activity that I really enjoyed. I'd found an outlet to transfer my inner most buried emotions and thoughts on and of the world. Through writing these speeches, I was able to connect to something within myself that allowed me to coherently form a common bond with my readers and listeners. I was able to connect with people who had similar passions, and together we were able to build greater platforms that dealt specifically with the intended problems.

When you base your speeches around the things you love, you will find yourself involved in more meaningful activities and developing healthy relationships with like-minded individuals. Things will start to fall in place. The right kind of people will begin to gravitate towards you, providing you with the necessary fuel to keep your passionate flame ignited. It will be beneficial to set aside at least an hour per day to invest some time and energy into speaking. Whether you choose to do it in front of friends or family members, or you can just practice in front of a mirror while imagining you have an audience.

The power you will gain from being an efficient speaker will change your whole outlook on life. You will begin to see the world in a whole new perspective. People will begin to look up to you as if you are a God or Goddess. With your words, you will have the power to build or destroy, give or take, love or hate. What you do for and with yourself will depend on what you *think* of yourself. If you think you can make the world a better place through expressing your passion, you will. Maybe you just want to change *your* life. Whatever it is that you desire, you will obtain. If all you want or need is to overcome your fear of speaking in public, you will achieve that by the time you are done practicing.

Using all of the methods I've recommended in *Speaking Potion*, you will be able to network, collaborate, influence, and evaluate others. As long as you based your speeches on things you are knowledgeable and passionate about, you will always have a promising path to success. Your passion can carry a positive energy that is so addictive, people who wouldn't normally be interested in anything outside themselves will begin to pay attention. Once you have someone's attention, you can change their hearts, minds, motives, and perceptions.

Some of the benefits of being an effective public speaker are: wealth, money, material possessions, dominance, control over others, enjoyments of life, and the power to influence anyone to do anything. The power to make a major impact on the world. These benefits can be a gift if possessed by the right person. A curse if possessed by the wrong person. Which one are you?

If your intention is to use your public speaking powers for evil, please promptly return your copy of *Speaking Potion* for a full refund. I do not want it on my conscious that I've helped to create a monster. We already have enough of those in the world. But if you are intending on using your powers for good, make sure you own a physical copy of *Speaking Potion* and register atwww.SpeakingPotion.com to be an invited guest at our fifth year anniversary celebration. My goal is to help five million people overcome their fear of public speaking and for those five million people to each help at least five others each. I believe the more people are able to communicate and express their feelings, the easier it will become to find solutions to some of life's problems.

I believe speaking is the most valuable commodity anyone can possess in this world. Through speaking, we are able to make our life as easy or as hard as possible. Speaking opens doors for people that would normally remain closed. Speaking creates the magical dance between men and women that makes them form a union and produce an abundance of children to populate our wonderful world. You will find, in every society, it is the men and women with the power to speak that are held at high prestige. Physical strength ruled in the times of uncivility. In our modern civilized times of technological advancement, the tongue is mightier than the sword.

One can cause more damage with words than they can with a fist or cause more happiness with words than they can with a kiss. I say this because good speakers are valuable at any event. As an effective speaker, you can turn someone's curses into blessings, nightmares into daydreams. You can use motivating words to shine the brightest lights on their darkest paths. You can tap into their soul with words that are worth more than a pound of gold. Words give us superpowers that can only be used when and if we choose to use them.

Take a moment and think about all of the things that a person can make happen just by using words. A word of command can break down a wall, a word of hate can create a war. A word of love can promote unity, a word of security can help keep together a community. A word of survival can cause soldiers to load up their rifles, a word of miracle can cause church goers to cling onto their bibles. A word of peace can cause destruction to desist, a word of power can cause people to persist. *You* are filled with words that you control and are able to use for the benefit of converting your passion into an instrument of profits.

Words are a resource that are as valuable as diamonds, gold, water, food, and even oil. The fact that there are people who are making millions of dollars from being public speakers is enough to tell you that speaking is a business. The same way that people get hungry for food or thirsty for beverages is the same way they get a need to talk or be talked to. Verbal communication stimulates a part of our brain that gives us a feeling of self-importance, self-worth. For this reason, people go to church, school, bars, clubs, concerts, or any place where they can receive the perpetual messages that make them feel alive.

Words are so powerful that sometimes all it takes is just *one* to get your message across. Senator Barack Obama was a Community Organizer before he got deeper into politics, which means he already had a passion for the people's problems. He knew what they wanted, needed, and how to speak to them to get their votes. When Obama was running for president of the United States, his one message was the word "hope." The word hope is so powerful that you can build a whole book filled with thousands of pages around it or give a five-hour speech based on the word hope. And when Obama became the 44th president of the United States, his inauguration in Washington D.C. was the largest audience that any president had ever received. It was a monumental moment in history.

Had Obama not been able to convert his passion into the political realm, his attempts to help better the quality of life of his constituents would not have been as fruitful. He flourished because he was driving in a familiar lane that he was comfortable with and had, to a certain extent, mastered. He effortlessly won the election by using a word he knew everyone wanted to hear: hope.

You, too, have a word related to your passion that you can use to help propel your career as a public speaker. Ask yourself, "If I could describe *myself* in just one word, what would that word be?" If you had to write an essay on why that one word is the representation of you, how many pages would your essay be? Would you be able to write a five-hundred-page book on the one word that represents you? Would you be able to talk to an audience for two hours on why that word resonates with who you are?

If you don't know the answers, it's okay. If you have not yet found a word that represents your passion in life, that's okay, too. This is what the speaking potion is for: to help you find yourself and develop your abilities to their intended heights. There are no obstacles you aren't able to overcome, no limits you can't reach. Anything in life you want is yours to have. The way you go about getting it is the only determining factor on whether you get to keep it or not. The things that you work hard to achieve and obtain will last longer than what was given or taken. You have the power to create your world by following your dreams and allowing your passion to lead you to your purpose.

The life that you want for yourself in your mind can become the life you live in reality. Don't allow past mistakes and accidents to keep you stagnant. Don't allow the passion fuel that's steadily burning within you to ever die out. You were born barefoot. If you have to move forward barefoot, then do it.

Joe: "Now, tell me, Jen. What have you learned?"

Jen: "So, if I follow my dream and allow my passion in life to be my compass, I can live happily?"

Joe: "Well, isn't happiness everyone's ultimate goal in life? Why should we have to fight for something that we already own?"

Jen: "I understand perfectly, Joe. Being disconnected from my passion can cause me to lead a miserable life. That's why I must plant seeds pertaining to the things that I am passionate about."

Joe: "Exactly. And if you being the spokesperson for Vain Apparel is something you have a passion for, then go for it and be the greatest spokesperson they've ever had."

Jen: "I do love fashion, Joe. Ever since I was a young girl, I'd dream of one day starting my own clothing company for women of all shapes and sizes. Maybe I'll start my presentation by telling the audience about myself. What do you think?"

Joe: "I think you're ready to move on to chapter six."

Jen: "Why is that? What's chapter six about?"

Joe: "Recognizing your audience."

Jen: "What do you mean? Like looking around to see if there are any famous people in the audience before I start speaking?"

Joe: "No, not exactly, but maybe I should have added that when I was writing the chapter."

Jen: "Okay, well, why don't I just be quite and listen while you tell me all I need to know from chapter six."

Joe: "Hey, would you like to come over to my place and we can finish the book together? I'll call you an Uber."

Jen: "I don't know, baby, maybe after chapter six, depending on how I'm feeling."

· CHAPTER 6 ·

RECOGNIZE YOUR AUDIENCE

One of the most important skills to have as a public speaker is the ability to recognize your audience so you know what it will take to maintain their attention throughout your speech. If you want to grab and keep their attention, you are going to have to be able to speak their language—and I don't mean their native tongue. I'm talking about their slang, jargon.

If you are speaking to a group of children on the importance of not smoking, you wouldn't want to use words and phrases like, "According to the Surgeon General, daily consumption of nicotine can decrease your life span astronomically." With that type of speech, you'll be lucky if *you* don't fall asleep. You might even trigger your audience members' need to leave the room for a smoke.

It is critical that you learn the slang/jargon of the group you are speaking to so you can make your speech relatable. Depending on the age of your audience, you might want to go as far as dressing like them in order to get your message across. Make sure you do some research. Surf the internet. If you know the exact location of where you'll be giving the speech, visit the neighborhood ahead of time to get a feel for the environment.

Knowing your audience is like knowing yourself. Although people tend to be unpredictable creatures, there are certain things you can almost always expect people to do. Why? Because you have those same expectations, certain natural reactions, in yourself. If you hear a funny joke, you are naturally going to react with a laugh. If someone makes a sudden outburst during a moment of silence, your natural reaction will be to jump or look around to see where the noise came from. Knowing that about yourself, it's safe to expect others to react in the same manner.

When faced with the task of presenting a speech in front of a group of people you're not familiar with, or don't know much about, the safest thing to do is aim for universal reactors. In a room of a thousand people, even if only six hundred of them reacted the way you wanted them to, you've done your job.

You are never going to make everyone happy. You're never going to make everyone laugh. But if you can cheer up most of the people you come across, then you are on the right path. Your audience should always be the most important thing about your speech. It's as if "the customer is always right." Pretend your audience are your customers. The better you know them, the easier it will be for you to control them. When you are up there, away from the crowd, behind the podium, or on that stage, you need to be in total control of the situation. Knowing your audience puts you in control, and gives them a sense of camaraderie, trust, and security. You want to be able to build a connection with them that will last way after you're done giving your speech. The same people that came to hear you speak on one topic might just show up for the next.

When you know your audience, you will be able to recognize them in situations outside of the public speaking arena. Parts of you will always be with them. This theory doesn't apply to every public speaker, only the great ones. A great public speaker is what you should aim to become. Great public speakers always have a way of leaving a lasting impression on their audience. Most do this by having their own personal catchphrase.

Daytime TV talk show host Wendy Williams is the perfect example of someone who knows her audience. She is a master at what she does and her ability to communicate, connect, and control her audience is phenomenal. She is one of the only TV hosts to get up out her chair and go into the audience to shake her "cohosts'" hands during every commercial break. This solidifies her as a people person, someone who doesn't place her status as a talk show host above her audience members.

Wendy even has her own catchphrase, which adds to her memorability. Whenever any audience member gets a chance to have Wendy place her microphone in front of their face, the first thing you will hear come out of the audience member's mouth is Wendy's catchphrase: "How you doin'?" This has become a mandatory greeting for any and everyone that steps foot on the Wendy Williams Show, whether a guest or an audience member. To repeat the catchphrase is to let not only Wendy, but the rest of the audience, know you are one of them. You are reaffirming to everyone watching that you've taken the pledge, and that you are down for the cause.

Knowing your audience prepares you for dealing with events that are unpredictable and people who are unstable. This is why you will see a number of bodyguards nearby whenever a politician is giving a speech. In these types of unpredictable events there are no real connections between the speaker and the audience. The speaker is attempting to sell himself or herself as a product of the people's desire. There are no guarantees that the people will accept what they're being told as truth. The uncertainty can turn a peaceful event into a demonstration.

That type of scenario is much more liable to happen when in the presence of people who are emotionally unstable. Being that politics can cause emotional distress to a person who is sensitive about their party's agenda, the wrong word, phrase, argument, or suggestion can cause them to lash out at the speaker. This is one of the many potential outcomes of publicly speaking in front of an audience that you may not know.

The best way to avoid any disturbance during your speech or presentation is to make sure you know your audience. Even when you think you do, certain things can occur that will always be out of your control. If someone is in the audience for the sole purpose of causing a disturbance, there is nothing you can do to stop them. When you are in the presence of audience members that you do know, you will be able to count on them to protect you from any unsolicited threats. If you are giving a speech in a large room of about 200 people and someone becomes disrespectful or throws a shoe at you, you want to be able to know that your audience will escort the person out of the building if you tell them to.

President Donald J. Trump is a perfect example of someone that knows his audience. As a political figure, one will always encounter oppositions at rallies or assemblies whenever he or she has to deliver a speech to a crowd. There are two types of ways that most people show their opposition. One is using placard signs that expresses their feelings. That is a form of **soft opposition**. Alternatively, they shout, scream, yell, and cry out their disapproval of the person that is speaking. That type is called **hard opposition**.

At one of Mr. Trump's rally, about a year after winning the election to become President of the United States, there were many soft oppositions in the audience, waving their placard signs around to be televised for the world to see. But what made the news that night was the hard opposition coming from a man in the crowd who'd caused such a ruckus, some of President Trump's supporters took it upon themselves to escort the trouble maker from the audience. The President encouraged his audience and praised them for intervening on his behalf. They were able to remove the man without incident.

Now *that* is the power of knowing your audience. Although I'm sure there were many security teams present at the rally, Mr. Trump didn't have to rely on his security. He knew his audience enough to feel safe among them. He knew that by any means necessary, they would put their lives on the line to protect him from any possible threat. As a public speaker you want to have that same relationship with the people you are trying to get your message to. You want for them to believe in you so much they will not allow anything or anyone to get in the way of your message being heard. No matter what it is you are speaking about, you have to understand that the people in your audience are the potion that gives you your energy to keep on going.

Knowing the people you are addressing raises your levels of confidence, security, knowledge, and ability to connect with them. You want your audience to see themselves when they look at you. You want them to think that they're listening to their own thoughts when they hear you speak. You want them to feel as if they've eaten a full course meal, not a snack, after hearing you speak. You want them to really know you.

When faced with the task of speaking in front of an audience you know nothing about, there are tactics you can use to win them over. You have to plant the seed at the beginning of your speech. The best way to start any form of public speaking, whether in front of family, friends, or strangers, is by using a quote from a popular song, movie, or famous person. You can also begin by using humor and even self-mockery to demystify certain news and entertain your audience. When you tell jokes, be careful because there's always a chance that not everyone will get it or that some people will get offended. You can start with an anecdote about a personal story of your life that people might be able to relate to. Start off with a profound question that will make everyone think.

Once you decide how to start your speech, make sure that it is informative, attention-grabbing, crystal clear, and to the point. As you are speaking, use all of your senses to analyze the audience and keep tabs on their responses. You want to know how they are responding to what you are saying so you can improve your speech. Sometimes when you write a speech specifically for a topic and you know all of your points, there are times you might have to improvise to make sure you are connecting with your audience. Your main focus should always be getting to know them.

You can get away with a lot of mistakes when you know your audience. If you happen to relay some wrong information while giving a speech and someone corrects you, you can turn it into a humorous moment and your audience will be delighted to have the pleasure of laughing it off with you. In fact, making a mistake once in a while can greatly work in your favor. After all, it just proves that you are a human being like everyone else.

As long as you're not giving a speech on a topic like performing heart surgery, in a room full of medical students, or on anything dealing with life and death situations, your audience members are like your cheerleaders. The more you can engage them in your presentation, the more positive energy they will respond with. You'll need all the positive energy you can get to fuel the engine that moves your train of thoughts. The right reaction from an audience can trigger an undiscovered interest within you that motivates you to transform.

Some of us walk through life not knowing what we want, or what we are able to give back. Public speaking is one of the many ways you can realize who you are and what your purpose in life is. Because of the connection we all share as human beings, sometimes one can receive answers from another while delivering a message based on one's own life.

I don't mean receiving advice from someone, though—more like receiving life. Many people exist without knowing their purpose. One of the many reasons is because they don't take the time to get to know themselves or others. Become your own audience. Know yourself. When you know yourself, you know your purpose, your destiny, your aim. Anyone that chooses to come hear you speak will come with an understanding of why they are there. Churchgoers go to church to hear the words of God. They have an understanding of who is preaching to them and what it is that they expect to hear. Imagine going to church one Sunday to hear your pastor, priest, rabbi, or imam speaking about everything that is going on in the political world and nothing spiritual. If that became a natural occurrence, it might be enough to make you switch churches (or religions).

That is why you must always recognize your audience and be able to recognize yourself. Your message to any specific audience should be solid, never flexible—especially when it is something that you believe in wholeheartedly. More people will respect you when you stick to your guns than when you allow yourself to become influenced by the desires of the majority. Remember: if you had built your audience on the premise of them following you because of your willingness to stand your ground, straying from that will only cause you to lose them. Be true to yourself and those who look up to you for guidance.

Having an audience solidifies your position as a leader. If your purpose is to sell women's and men's clothes to your audience, you have to not only be a spokesperson of the brand, but also someone that wears the brand on a daily basis. You have to become a living example of what the brand represents. You have to make others see the brand every time they look at you or think of you. You have to build that bond with the people who will become your customers.

One of my favorite brand promoters is Kim Kardashian. Kim is the perfect example of someone who recognizes her audience. The reason so many people love her and watch the show is because she is always herself. She doesn't conform to the rules that put limits and restrictions on the behaviors of women. She does what she wants, how she wants to do it. Her audience loves her for that. She could've changed her image and catered to the more elite group of people in society, but instead, Kim chose to remain herself. She knows that a lot of people admire her for her body. Even after getting married to the rapper Kanye West and having a child, Kim still posed nude for magazines. She is comfortable with who she is, and she recognizes that her audience will respect her no matter what she chooses to do.

When you are able to achieve such levels of success in life, you are able to say things like, "I can shoot someone in broad day light on Fifth Avenue and not lose a fan." That is a bold statement for *anyone* to make. When you recognize your audience and they in turn recognize you, you can say and do almost anything and they will back you 100 percent. That is the type of loyalty you want to build as a public speaker.

You want your audience to trust and believe that whatever comes out your mouth has a perfect, logical explanation. Being that they are your audience, you do not have to explain yourself to them because they should already understand.

Joe: "This level of understanding stems from you knowing your audience as much as you know yourself. They are a part of you and you a part of them. Almost like how we are Jen."

Jen: "Aaawww, Joe, that is so sweet. It seems like you always know the right words to say, even in moments like this."

Joe: "I can't help it. When it comes to doing anything to help you out, I'm all in. I want to see you succeed as much as you want to succeed."

Jen: "So, is that offer still on the table?"

Joe: "What offer?"

Jen: "You know, to come over to your place so I can experience the visualization of 'Speaking Potion.'"

Joe: "Your Uber driver's name is Gregory. He will be there in about fifteen minutes to pick you up. And don't worry about it, it's already paid for."

Jen: "What! Are you kidding? When did you do that?"

Joe: "About twenty minutes after you told me you'll think about it. I texted him all the necessary information while we've been on the phone."

Jen: "Oh my gosh, Joe, you're something else. I guess I gotta go get ready now. I'll see you soon."

Joe: "I'm not letting you off the hook that easy. We still have lots of time left. Now tell me, what did you learn from—"

Jen: "Chapter six? I learned that to be able to maintain the attention of my audience I must always find a way to recognized who they are, what they're about, their likes and dislikes as a collective, if possible."

Joe: "Wow, great, Jen! You really do pay attention. I can't wait for you to get here so we can start chapter seven."

Jen: "What's chapter seven's title?"

Joe: "'Control Your Lips.' I'll see you soon—no, hold on. I just thought of something. I'll read while you get ready."

· CHAPTER 7 ·

CONTROL
YOUR LIPS

To fully understand the concept of becoming a great public speaker, one has to be receptive to all information obtained and be willing to put it to practice. Public speaking is more than just an act of verbal communication. To be successful at it, you have to utilize and master every aspect of your body language. You have to develop coordination, animation, endurance, gestures, movements, and mannerisms by which a person communicates. All that, and the pressure of having to stand or sit in front of a crowd of strangers to speak, can be overwhelming.

If you are truly dedicated to becoming a great public speaker and want to deliver your speeches without worrying about being able to perform when the time comes, you must learn how to control your respiratory system. When using your voice, you must treat it like you would treat any other tool. If you're a mechanic who uses a wrench to tighten nuts and bolts, you're going to want to keep that wrench well-oiled so it won't get rusty. The same goes for your voice box. Not only do you have to keep it lubricated, you have to know how to have control of your breathing.

To speak properly, you must know and learn how to breathe properly. Your lungs are the force that drives your vocal cords.

Anything that goes in or out of your body via the upper region must be pushed by your lungs. Speaking can be an arduous task; in public, it can become very embarrassing for anyone who doesn't have full control of their breathing. Knowing how to breathe correctly is the key to speaking with confidence and fluency.

You must learn about your respiratory system and how to navigate it in order to speak fluidly. A lot of people who have a problem with speaking in public will get to a certain point in their presentation and begin to feel choked up, sweaty, nervous, at a loss for words. You might even see them turn red in the face as they stand in front of a crowd. This is usually due to a lack of control over their breathing.

As a public speaker, you should make it your business to master your breathing. It can help to cleanse and purify your inner respiratory system. This system is the highway that your voice travels through whenever you need to get a message across. If you want your message to arrive clearly and accurately without any forms of interference, you have to make sure your highway is free of possible obstructions and pollutions. Be careful with what you put into your body. If you are filling up your respiratory system with all kinds of toxic chemicals, you will cause it to malfunction.

Once your respiratory system malfunctions, it will effect your; nasal passages, larynx, trachea, veins, arteries, bronchus, esophagus, throat, and when all of those systems are effected your ability to speak will deteriorate or completely shut down. Can you imagine preparing for a speech all week and the night before you give the speech, you go out with a few friends to a local bar and get drunk? What do you think will happen the next day when you have to wake up and go give your speech to a group of strangers?

If you can manage to have total control over your breathing, you just might do a good job (or, at least, a better job than someone who has no awareness of breathing techniques). Breathing is the life force that stabilizes your whole body, giving you control of your every action and reaction. This is why when someone is placed in a chokehold to prevent them from inhaling and exhaling, their natural response is to react erratically.

When you are about to give a speech, you want to be able to have control of your delivery. Knowing how to breathe the right way can put you in the position of a professional public speaker in the eyes of your audience. Take time before you begin speaking to exercise your lungs. This helps provide calmness and clarity. When air travels in and out of your lungs, your respiratory system comes alive as the air circulates. Before any words can come out of your mouth, they must go through the process of being approved by your respiratory system.

If your breathing is not right, you will not be able to properly formulate a sentence. Knowing how to breathe properly is an essential tool. It fuels your brain and improves respiratory functions, as well as the level of oxygen in your blood flow. I advise anyone who wants to become a public speaker to always start by speaking from the heart. The veins that your blood flow through are connected to your heart, which is connected to all the other parts of your respiratory system. When you speak from the heart, everything becomes synchronized. This will cause you to reduce anxiety, stress, and other mood disorders that can prevent you from speaking clearly to your audience.

Having control of your breathing determines whether you are a sprint or a marathon speaker. If your goal is to take this public speaking passion of yours to places unknown, then I would suggest you practice stabilizing your breathing. There are many exercises that you can do to train yourself on how to stay in control. I would suggest you begin by reciting some of your short speeches. Take a few minutes to just breathe in and out slowly through your nose. Make it a habit of yours to become better at controlling your breathing.

The goal is to have conscious control of your breathing so that your every thought will be in harmony with your words. The more aware you become of every breath that leaves your lungs, the more aware you will be of every thought that formulates in your mind. Every word that rolls off of your tongue. The benefits of using the breathing techniques are vital, helping you gain control of your mind and body. Any tension you have been experiencing will release itself into the universe.

The best thing about breathing techniques is that you can do them anywhere: at home, at the office, outdoors. Each time you practice your breathing, you will get better at it. Once you are able to control your breathing by using these exercises, you will no longer have to worry about sweating, trembling, stuttering, forgetfulness, nervousness, or any other symptoms that are usually displayed by people with fear of public speaking. Breathing techniques will calm your mind and body and hone the inner confidence that you already possess. You will receive the energy to fluidly speak as air circulates through your body.

You will begin to find your voice when you allow your breathing to become your oral compass. Not the voice that you speak with, but the voice that speaks through you—that deep-down-from-the-depths-of-your-belly-and-out-of-your-soul voice. The voice that's going to set you free to conquer your journey. It represents one thing and one thing only: the truth.

Crowds of people will come to hear you speak. Your words will vibrate the ground from under their feet like an earthquake because you will be speaking from the heart.

The power of speaking from the heart can become greater when you are in control of every breath you take to make your message resonate. No longer will you feel tense or agitated before or while speaking in front of people. Your ability to use your breathing techniques is like having a superpower that grows stronger and allows you to speak for longer durations. Even if you have to stop talking to take a breath every time, it will still work in your favor. How? Because as odd as it may seem, even silence can be a major key component in public speaking.

Think about it: what usually happens when someone takes a pause in the middle of speaking? Well, usually it grabs the attention of the people that weren't necessarily listening before. All they were hearing was noise, and then the noise stopped. Now they want to know why. Now is your chance to grab their attention. Recapture your audience by saying something profound. Taking a deep breath before opening your mouth to say anything can help to create a batch of fresh ideas. Each breath you take is like a burst of energy being transmitted directly to your brain within the matter of seconds. When you delay a breath, you make what you create fresh.

Being that your ability to effectively speak in public depends on the quality of your respiratory system, it's only right that you maintain its usefulness through daily training. Now this system is a muscle. Like every other muscle in your body, the more you exercise it, the more it grows and remains operable. Unlike your arms, legs, stomach, and chest, you don't have to go get a gym membership and spend hours weightlifting to make your breathing great. You simply have to be more mindful of the power that you are able to conjure through your breathing.

As far as exercises, you can do simple tasks like closing your eyes as you breathe in and out. Then, open them and take some full breaths in through your nose and out through your mouth. Doing this for about five to ten minutes per day can train your mind to become much more aware of your ability to use breath control whenever necessary. You don't have to partake in any intense exercises because all that will do is backfire by making your breathing very unsteady. Unsteady breathing leads to an unsteady mind.

Focus on relaxing your nervous system, by slowly inhaling and exhaling. Make sure you exhale slower than you inhale. You are training your body to relieve stress, even when you are not in a stressful situation. Remember, you are trying to grow a muscle to make it strong so that when you need to use it, it will be ready, willing, and capable to perform. Breath control exercises should be practiced at different times of the day and in different environments, such as crowded places among strangers where you can better prepare your mind for having to give a speech in a similar situation. If you live in the inner city, this is a good exercise to try on a crowded train during rush hour.

As a public speaker, you will want to give a tune-up to your respiratory system as many times as possible to keep it from being clogged up. Your nasal passages must remain free of obstructions at all times in order for air to flow freely, without transporting any defective particles to disrupt your breathing. This means you have to develop the habit of cleaning out your nostrils, keeping the passages free from mucus and dried up cells.

Next is your larynx, which is a long tube that is located, according to *Merriam Webster's Collegiate Dictionary*, at the "modified upper part of the trachea of air-breathing vertebrates that in humans, most other mammals, and a few lower forms contains the vocal cord." Being that a public speaker cannot function without his or her vocal cords intact, I would suggest drinking a lot of water and tea to keep your larynx moisturized at all times.

The trachea, which is the main tube in your respiratory system, should be given similar treatment. Both are the main air-carrying tubes. You should want to minimize the amount of stress that you place upon them. Shouting and screaming for hours will cause your voice to become hoarse, which would not fit right with any public speaker (unless it was their natural sounding voice). Clarity is the key to effectively getting your message across.

Now, your veins are what I would like to call the carriers. They are the vessel that transport your blood through your body's intricate networks to make connection with your heart. This, I believe, is why when someone speaks from their heart, their words give life to the topic of discussion and raises understanding.

With all of the motion that's going on within your body, none of it would be possible if it wasn't for your arteries. Although its functions are similar to the vein's, your artery, according to *Merriam Webster's Collegiate Dictionary*, is a "channel (as a river or highway) of transportation or communication; the main channel in a branching system." To anyone who wishes to become a great public speaker, that information should've translated to mean, "Your body is a vehicle and how far you go in life with it will be determined by the type of fuel you use." The food that you put into your body every day will either make you sluggish or give you energy. The more fattened food you eat, the slower it will take you to reach your goals. The healthier you eat, the faster you will get there.

Watch what you eat. As a public speaker, you are now responsible for the daily maintenance of your body. The more blood is allowed to circulate through your body and down your highway, the better you will feel, look, and speak. You don't want to cause any constriction of your air passages to the lungs. You want to be able to breathe right at all times. Your bronchus, esophagus, and throat are all equally responsible for making sure you deliver an eloquent speech.

Your voice sits on the throne of your throat, ready to talk your talk. If you haven't been treating yourself right, taking great care of your respiratory system, your body will tell on you. You will cough and sneeze excessively. You will overheat and begin to sweat while speaking to people. Your mind will wander off when spoken to, making it impossible for you to listen to anyone. The proper nutrition in your system will enhance the power of your speaking potion.

Joe: "Jen, Jen! Are you still on the phone I can't hear you breathe? You must be here then…. There you are. Are you alright? You look like you just ran a Martha Manhattan Marathon."

Jen: "Joe, what took you so long? I've been standing outside your door for the past—"

Joe: "Did you knock?"

Jen: "No. I thought you'd have a security camera system that sees me, notifies you, and voilà! The door opens."

Joe: "No, Jen, I haven't gotten that far into technology. All you had to do was knock and the door shall be opened."

Jen: "Well, I'm in aren't I?"

Joe: "Yes you are, and you look as beautiful as ever. How was the ride over? Everything went well?"

Jen: "Thanks for the compliment, and yes, everything went fine. Gregory was a gentleman. So, what's a Martha Manhattan Marathon?"

Joe: "Jen! You're a Manhattanite! But, oh, yeah. I keep forgetting you're new to the city. A Martha Manhattan Marathon is sponsored by Martha Stewart and Snoop Dogg, they host it. It brings awareness to victims of domestic abuse and gun violence. Every 23rd of July millions of families from all around the world travel to Manhattan to participate."

Jen: "Ooooh okay. I think I know what you're talking about now. The other day while listening to Z100, I heard something about the Obama's co-hosting a marathon in Manhattan. Maybe that's what they were talking about. Joe, I lost my breath walking up those steps. Your elevator isn't working."

Joe: "Maybe. But I'm glad you're here. Losing your breath is exactly what I want to talk to you about. Come have a seat. I'll get you a glass of water, unless you'd rather have something stronger?

Jen: "You're not going to try to Cosby me, are you, Joe?"

Joe: "Never. Nor will I play any music by R. Kelly."

Jen: "In that case, I'll have some champagne."

Joe: "Great choice. But before I pop the cork... What did you learn from chapter seven?"

Jen: "Lets see, chapter seven, 'Control Your Lips.' So, I must always remember the importance of breathing right and taking care of my respiratory system. I wish your elevator would've worked, that would've saved some unnecessary pressure on my respiratory system. But, most importantly, my lungs are my tool, or should I say my money-makers?"

Joe: "Looks like you've earned your glass of champagne. If I'm being honest, I didn't think you would catch everything I said."

Jen: "Why, because I was in the middle of getting ready while you were talking to me? Please, Joe, I know how to multi-task."

Joe: "I see. You sure did a fine job with your choice of apparel."

Jen: "Oh, this ol' thing! It's an Vain Apparel baby doll dress. It was given to me by the company. It cost a fortune. It's made out of 100 percent recycled plastic. Go ahead, touch it, see how smooth it feels."

Joe: "Wow, you're right. It does feel different. Can I try it on?"

Jen: "No, silly! But why don't we get started on chapter eight while we drink? I'll need to start heading back home in an hour."

Joe: "Alright then. Since you're in a rush, I'll speed things up. Chapter eight is called 'Align With Your Sign.' What's your zodiac sign, Jen?"

Jen: "Sagittarius. Why?"

Joe: "Here, have a drink. We're about to get into it right now."

· CHAPTER 8 ·

ALIGN WITH
YOUR SIGN

Astrologically speaking, what is your birth sign? Are you an Aries, Taurus, Gemini, Cancer, Leo, Virgo, Libra, Scorpio, Sagittarius, Capricorn, Aquarius, or a Pisces? The reason I ask is because whether you know it or not *you* have the natural abilities of a great public speaker embedded in your astrological DNA. You share a special kind of connection to some of the greatest speakers that have ever faced a crowd and captivated them with the right *words*.

For every sign, I will name some known famous people that *you* share your natural gift of public speaking with:

Aries: David Letterman and Sarah Jessica Parker.

Taurus: Dwane "The Rock" Johnson and Janet Jackson.

Gemini: Mario Cuomo, Che Guevara, Tupac Shakur, Kanye West, Donald J. Trump, Angelina Jolie, Marilyn Monroe, Joan Rivers, and Paula Abdul.

Cancer: Alexander the Great, Nelson Mandela, George W. Bush, Lena Horne, Lindsey Lohan, and Nancy Reagan.

Leo: Napoleon Bonaparte, Benito Mussolini, Fidel Castro, Robert De Niro, Magic Johnson, Barack H. Obama, Bill Clinton, Monica Lewinsky, Madonna, Martha Stewart, and Kathie Lee Gifford.

Virgo: Michael Jackson, Regis Philbin, John McCain, Leo Tolstoy, Queen Elizabeth I, Mother Teresa, and Cameron Diaz.

Libra: Jesse Jackson, Simon Cowell, Will Smith, Kelly Ripa, Gwyneth Paltrow, and Serena Williams.

Scorpio: Johnny Carson, Walter Cronkite, Bill Gates, Billy Graham, Hillary Rodham Clinton, Condoleezza Rice, Whoopi Goldberg, and Demi Moore.

Sagittarius: Dale Carnegie, Winston Churchill, Jamie Foxx, Jay-Z, Frank Sinatra, Miley Cyrus, Tyra Banks, Jane Fonda, and Britney Spears.

Capricorn: Martin Luther King Jr., Joseph Stalin, J. Edgar Hoover, Richard M. Nixon, Elvis Presley, Denzel Washington, Dianne Sawyer, Katie Couric, and Ellen Degeneres.

Aquarius: Ted Koppel, Franklin D. Roosevelt, Tom Brokaw, Dr. Dre, John Grisham, Chris Rock, George Stephanopoulos, Oprah Winfrey, Alicia Keys, Angela Davis, Paris Hilton, and Jennifer Aniston.

Pisces: Albert Einstein, George Washington, Steve Jobs, Shaquille O'Neal, Elizabeth Taylor, Ruth Bader Ginsburgh, Dr. Seuss, and Carrie Underwood.

You can achieve the same, if not higher, level of success than anyone that you happen to share your birth sign with. Remember, we are all connected in one way or another. If you know what connects you with someone, it is easy to tap into their energy and take from them what you need in order to fit it into your life's puzzle. You are not doing a bad thing by taking it from them because part of their purpose in life is to serve others, especially people that are of the same sign as themselves. We unconsciously do this all the time. It's essential to our survival and beneficial to our evolution.

As children we took from our parents and siblings, and as we got older we begin to take from our friends, neighbors, and environments. Like the air we breathe, what we take is never missing because it's always there. It recycles, replenishes, refreshes. It is a source set forth by the universe to be used by those of us that are aware of its existence. *You* are now aware of its existence. Therefore, it is your duty to take full advantage of its powers. As you travel on your journey to become the world's greatest public speaker, be inspired, motivated by those that share your birth sign.

The reason I added both males and females for each sign is because all of the astrological signs are associated with either a masculine or feminine attribute. Six are associated with masculine; the other six are feminine. Whether you are a male that falls under a feminine attribute or a female that falls under a masculine attribute doesn't mean that you are or were meant to be the opposite sex. It just means that you have a strong connection with that side. There are successful people that shares your qualities.

Be proud of those that you're connected with astrologically. You are an extension of them, as they are an extension of you. Maybe you didn't know before that you shared some of the same character traits as some men and women of greatness. Well, now you do. By the time you're done reading this chapter, you should be able to tap into your own greatness. What kind of impact will you make on the world? How will you represent for your birth sign? Which one of the twelve signs do you get along with the most?

For each of the twelve astrological signs, there are certain character traits that you already have within you that can enable you to become a great public speaker. As an individual that was nurtured in a different environment than some of the people who you share a sign with, you will be bringing something different to the scene. Your speech, mannerisms, and outlooks on things are all critical tools that can be used by you to differentiate your style of public speaking. Lucky for you you're on the developing stage, which means your biggest obstacle right now is learning how to be comfortable being yourself. You are your trademark. Once you can master speaking in front of different types of crowds, you can then start to take on the traits of others. You don't have to possess all twelve traits. Just one.

Mastering your own is the only thing that matters. To be mobile in life and get to your destination, sometimes it's easier if you travel light. The more baggage you take on, the harder it becomes for you to get to your destination. Anyone that is reading *Speaking Potion* is considered to be on the highway of life's most magical journey. And when you are traveling on that journey, it's a mandatory requirement that you possess at least one of the following qualities. If none apply to you, feel free to write to me personally to demand a refund. How many do you possess?

1: Intense and passionate

2: Brave, beautiful, benevolent

3: Courageous

4: Devoted and protective

5: Analytical, assertive, ambitious, artistic, adaptable

6: Charming, creative, compassionate, conscientious

7: Devoted, disciplined, determined

8: Energetic, easygoing, enthusiastic, exuberant

9: Friendly, fun, focused, freespirited, imaginative

10: Original, persistent, patient, receptive, steadiness, witty

If you possess one or more of these qualities, there is no reason why you shouldn't want to use it/them to your advantage. All it takes is for you to strengthen the quality(ies) you have in your possession and master it. Each quality that you possess represents a weapon at your disposal—let's say a sword. You have to sharpen your swords so they are effective. That way, when you use them, they will provide the desired effect. If you are a passionate person, you have to use that passion to speak on the subject that brings out your passion naturally without having to force anything. If it's meant for you to cry, you will naturally begin to shed tears in front of your audience. They will know that its real.

Feed from the energy of those that share the same birthday and sign as you. Allow your God-given gift to be shared with the rest of the world. Your gift entitles you to attain a position in life that is similar or greater than the most superior people representing your sign. You may not have received the same education as him or her. That doesn't matter. What matters is: if you are a Pisces like Shaquile O'neal, or a Gemini like Tupac Shakur, or a Scorpio like Demi Moore; *you* have the ability to publicly express yourself as good as, if not better than, them. Why? Because you share a trait with them that can be cultivated. Once you are able to see and understand this trait, you will come to understand yourself a lot more.

This hidden power that you possess can cause supernatural things to happen in your life, if used the right way and for the right purposes. The power is already within your core and ready for you to use it. If you don't use it, you will lose it. Once it's lost, it may take you a lifetime before you can find it again. So right now ,while you are in this state of self-elevation, you have to use all the forces at your disposal to get you to where you need to go. The rest of your fellow astrological sign members are rooting for you to make it up there with them.

Aries, use your energetic and aggressive character traits to speak to the hearts of those that are lacking speaking guidance. Allow your optimistic views to bring hope to those that aren't as inclined to think of the most favorable thoughts. Plant seeds of optimism with your eloquent words of wisdom. The same admiration that you so love to receive from others? Give it freely in the same volume that you would like to receive.

Taurus, you are one of the luckiest signs when it comes to being a public speaker. Why? Because most Taurus' have a beautiful speaking and singing voice, so that puts you ahead in the race with all the other signs. If you really want to become a great public speaker, you can—but you will have to do something about your stubbornness. Don't let that one negative trait become an obstacle to you achieving your goal. Humble yourself; speak up about the things that matter the most to you.

Gemini, the world is yours when it comes to being a public speaker. Why? Because naturally you are extremely verbal and intellectual. You are known for imposing your views on others. If you are having a problem with speaking in public it is only because of the subject matter. Once you are able to speak on topics that you're passionate about, it will take an army to stop you. You can arouse a lot of anger in others. You are a person that is known for not biting your tongue. When you speak, you speak with the authority of a god or goddess. Your chameleon ways allows you to change views when beneficial, but overall you are a natural orator with the ability to lead a nation.

Cancer, when it comes to being a public speaker, your strengths are in matters of the heart. Because you are sensitive, you're able to feel the pain of others and are receptive to different suggestions and ideas that can help you come up with solutions to problems.

Your joyful nature among friends and family can be converted to an audience that comes to watch you speak. Your hardened exterior can cause others to think twice about approaching you. For those who do, they are rewarded with your soft and friendly nature. As a public speaker you will do best as a public advocate.

Leo, you might be considered the king of the jungle. In the public speaking world you are a God. I'm not just saying this because I'm a Leo—I'm saying it because Leos possess qualities that are essential for public speaking. Leos are creative individuals. It takes that quality to write good speeches that you will have to recite in front of an audience. Enthusiastic is another great quality that leos possess. It is needed in order to keep a crowd on their feet. Bravery, is also a great quality to have. When your in front of a rough crowd that doesn't want to hear what you have to say, you have to be brave in order to go on delivering your message. So if you're a Leo, there is no limit to where you can go with being a public speaker.

Virgo, as a public speaker you need to be very cautious in what you say. Your critical tongue and sometimes unemotional attitude can give off the wrong message. I would suggest that you always write what you're about to speak on before speaking in a public forum. If you are interested in being a political radio host, I believe you will do great. Your knack for seeking to know and understand things will help towards maintaining an audience of like-minded individuals and those who are curious. Blogging might be another avenue you may want to experiment with. Nevertheless, you would make a very strong, passionate, and interesting public speaker.

Libra, you are magical when it comes to speaking in public. For you I made up the word "Libracadabra." Your power of charm is so magnetic, you can attract anyone with a beating heart. You are one of the signs that other signs look up to when it comes to being able to express yourself in public. You are a natural, socially-inclined, artistic, active person that is destined for greatness. If you choose public speaking as a career, you will most likely succeed.

Scorpio, your wild imagination can sometimes transform you into the characters that you create. This is a great character trait to possess. If you choose to imagine that you are the greatest public speaker in the world, you will make others believe it. Your ability to be persistent is another trait that can help make you a great public speaker. People get comfortable with what they've become familiar with.

Sagittarius, your sign is that of a centaur shooting an arrow. What that tells me about you is that you are a straight shooter. Match that with your energetic trait, the public speaking world is in need of people like yourself. Your freedom-loving nature can be useful in a camp counselor setting, working with children.

Capricorn, you are one of the many signs that is held in high regards to positions involving the government. Being a person who appreciate privacy, silence, and secrecy, you would be very valuable as an FBI agent or in any form of law enforcement. If in the armed forces you will be a great drill sergeant. Definitely a boss type.

Aquarius, your unconventional ways can sometimes land you in trouble, especially when you are around eccentric individuals which you seem to always attract. If you decide to become a public speaker, I would suggest that you cater your message to those groups because they will take to you like bees to honey.

Pisces, if you're thinking about becoming a public speaker to lead a congregation or become a lawyer, or any type of public advocate *do it*. You were born to be a leader. You possess some qualities that are essential and every other sign would kill for. Your receptiveness and intuition makes you a spiritually aware soul. You have the power to change the lives of others because people value your opinion on things. As a public speaker, you can lead a movement with your speech.

Jen: "A movement, huh! Well, if things don't work out as a camp counselor for me, I'm going to start a movement for women's rights and free education for every child across the world."

Joe: "Very noble of you. I, myself, am involved in a few humanitarian causes: The Human Deportation Project, Relief Activities for Earthquake Victims in Haiti, and I volunteer at Red Cross, FEMA, and where ever help is needed."

Jen: "Wow, Joe. Ever since I've known you, you've always been getting involved in humanitarian causes. Why?"

Joe: "Well, Jen, because that's the type of stuff I'm passionate about, and it is the only time I get to Align With My Sign. And speaking of—"

Jen: "I know, I know. What have I learned from chapter eight? Well, being that I'm a Sagittarius, I can achieve the same goals as Miley Cyrus, Tyra Banks, Dale Carnegie, or Jay-Z. We are all connected. It's up to me to align myself with like-minded people to receive the necessary energy I need to succeed."

Joe: "I'll toast to that. Want another drink?"

Jen: "Sure. But Joe, I have to ask you something."

Joe: "Shoot."

Jen: "Actually, I have to ask you two things. What is the favor you need? And I'm dying to know *what happened to Michelle?* Did she get to buy her dad the tie?"

Joe: "I'll tell you what Jen, if you will read the next chapter to me while I sit back and admire your beauty, I'll tell you when we're done reading 'Speaking Potion.'"

Jen: "Stop it, Joe, you're making me blush. Okay, I'll read. Do you mind if I take off my shoes to get more comfortable?"

Joe: "Not at all. As a matter of fact, I'll take them off for you."

Jen: "Thanks, that's so nice of you."

Joe: "Allow me the pleasure of relieving your feet from their high heel prison camp."

Jen: "Your such a gentleman, Joe. I'm glad I came over. We work great together—as a team, I mean, with you talking and me listening. And now me talking and you listening."

Joe: "Sometimes I feel as if you were made specially for me. It's almost like there's a version of you living in my head processing my every thought."

Jen: "What did I do now?"

Joe: "You've made it easy for us to transition to chapter nine, 'Be the "I" in Team.'"

Jen: "That sounds kind of selfish, Joe."

Joe: "Sometimes life requires you to be selfish in order to have enough to share."

Jen: "I don't know where this is going, but it sounds interesting."

Joe: "You'll enjoy the ride. I promise. After all, you're the one who'll be doing the driving. I'm just a passenger on the Jen-Juice Express."

Joe: "Well in that case, strap on your seatbelt, buddy. I'm about to transform into Danica Patrick."

Joe: "Okay, well, don't be afraid to stop and ask for directions if you happen to need any. That's what I'm here for."

Jen: "Thanks, Joe. Maybe later on after we arrive at our destination, I can show you what I'm here for."

Joe: "Okay then, pretty lady. Let's get going."

Jen: "I'm going to read chapter nine to you in my Marilyn Monroe voice."

Joe: "And I'll give you a foot massage while I listen."

· CHAPTER 9 ·

BE THE "I" IN TEAM

Do you get along well with others? Are you a team player? Can you find the "I" in team? If not, learn to be a team player and find the "I" in team. Many people like to believe that there is no "I" in team, but that just means that they aren't looking hard enough. The key to finding the "I" in team is just like everything else in life. You have to first look for it within. In team there are an "M" and an "E," and the ME is what you should take away from team in order to improve the "I."

Don't get me wrong, there is nothing wrong with being a team player. In fact, I encourage you to go out there and join any team activities that spark your interest. Joining different teams will enable you to have access to audiences of your peers at all times. Sometimes the best way to overcome the fear of speaking in public is by participating in sports or any extra-curricular activities that allow you to socialize, analyze, and voice your opinion within an organized group setting.

There is no better place than a room filled with like-minded individuals for you to take chances with an audience. You will be less prone to make mistakes. If you do you can always laugh it off and no one will hold it against you. They will, instead, help to correct you and probably will feel honored to do it. That is one of the benefit of being a team player: since everyone's goal on a team is to win, they will make sure to help you strengthen your weakness so that your efforts will be much more beneficial towards achieving the end goal. Although some people might perceive you to be a follower, don't worry about it. Some of the greatest leaders in the world were once followers. Just don't ever forget you're only following the team to get to the "I."

When you conquer the "I," you will be able to look at yourself in the mirror and say things like, "I am the baddest. I am the boldest. I am the most fearless. I am the greatest. I can turn my dreams into realities, my weaknesses into strengths. I can use my words to move mountains. Travel through different dimensions with every breath. Cause the earth to quake with every step. I am the voice of those who've wept, the eyes of those who've cried, the blood of those who've fought and died, speaking the thoughts of those with illimitable minds. I am delivered, I am delighted, I am devined. I am the evolution of mankind. The explosion of landmines. The wheel that spins the hands of time.

"There will be none but me, for I am the everlasting energy, the world's only true currency, philosophy, astrology, unity, and democracy. I am the speaker of truth, justice, and equality. I am the master of my mental-script. The driver of my destiny. My words are like rivers that run through the desert with the impact of a hurricane. I shall rain waves down on your brain with thunderous speech. When I speak, my verbal tone is like a cyclone, as I ride you up and down and all around, to keep you off your feet. My words shine like the moon, sweeter than honeycombs, more harmonious than virgin wombs. Whether in a stadium or a classroom, I will fight my fears 'til I rule. Look at my audience with a smile, 'cause I'm cool.

"In the middle of the storm I'm calm and full of passion. I know changes only come with action. It's time for me to make miracles happen. My mouth's a weapon, I'll use it to turn cursings into blessings, as I keep on advancing. With my fears I'm now dancing, laughing and joking, as I'm locked in arms with my oppositions. I have to remind myself every now and again, I'm in this to *win*. I am in this to *win*! All *I* need is my speaking potion, my speaking potion, my speaking potion...."

I wrote that as a short motivational poem, speech, mantra, or song, depending on the mood I'm in or the audience I'm in front of. I find it to be very helpful in building up my confidence before I have to give a speech, or whenever I just want to remind myself that *I* got this. Reciting the "Speaking Potion Poem" has become a daily practice of mine when I wake up with the feeling of uncertainty, as to whether or not I'll be able to deliver an Impromptu speech if a situation arises.

For those of you that might not know what an impromptu speech is: it's improvising, coming up with a speech on the spur of the moment without being prepared or aware you would have to give a speech. It's sort of like being in church and. out of nowhere, getting asked to speak on a problem that's been effecting the congregation or the community. Usually, you would be asked to speak because the congregation knows you're an eloquent speaker; however, when you're not prepared and the topic is something you're not familiar with, it can become a great challenge.

If ever you are faced with such a challenge, I would encourage you to search your mental database for the "Speaking Potion Poem" file and recite it to yourself as you are about to begin speaking on any topic. By motivating yourself to take on the challenge, you will clear out any fearful thoughts that might've been trying to deter you from taking advantage of the opportunity to speak. Remember: it is your duty to speak whenever called upon. As a public speaker, you have to continually practice your craft with as many different types of audiences as possible. That is the only way to make it to the top with the rest of the great public speakers of the world. You want that kind of recognition because you deserve it.

You want to one day be mentioned with the likes of those who are able to fill football stadiums with people that come to hear them speak. You have a message that needs to be heard by as many people as the next man or woman. You are important to the world; your life and experiences matters. Your truth needs to be heard, and others need to hear it so that they can feel free to speak theirs. A lot of the problems in and with the world can be resolved and solved by the simple act of speaking.

Speaking is the most powerful form of communication there is. What can make it even more powerful is when the speaker is speaking about his or her own experiences. The simple fact that you are being personal with your speech makes it impossible for anyone to challenge you. What you have been through in life are your own personal unique experiences, how you choose to react to certain events, how you responded to certain questions, and what you've said in certain situations are all uniquely *you*.

Before you developed this uniqueness, you had to watch and learn the correct response from many others. In a sense, we—as human beings—are always inadvertently part of a team. While some of us are aware of this fact, most of us are not. Have you ever heard the saying, "It takes a village to raise a child?" It is a true statement. For a child to learn its way around in the world, he or she must take on the characteristics and traits of almost everyone. In order for the "I" to survive in the world, one must put on many hats until you come across the right fit—but every hat you wear serves its purpose in the end. The main goal is to evolve as you live and learn from everyone and everything in your environment.

Have you ever heard the saying, "Teamwork makes the dream work?" If you have, what is the first question that comes to your mind when you hear it? For me it's, "Whose dream?" We all can't be having the exact same dream. There will have to be some deviation within the team. No matter how much we are all on the same page about performing to our maximum capacity in order to reach our desired goals, everyone has their own unique idea of what they want the ending to look like.

Teamwork is nothing more than a group of people who have decided to pool their resources together in order to become much more effective at attaining a desired result. Everyone involved has a different motive for why their team should win. Usually it will revolve around a personal agenda. So, in essence, "teamwork makes the dream work" is really just a motivational phrase used to fuel an individual's motor. One has to have some form of an investment in a team in order to want it to succeed. One has to have a dream of their own that can only become a reality through their participation in the team before they'll subscribe to the "teamwork makes the dream work" mentality.

Although you are part of the team, it is still about the ME. You are still working for the benefit of the "I." As long as you are able to recognize what you're doing, you can do it effectively. When you are a part of a team, you should make it your business to learn the strengths of all your team mates. Why? Because their strengths are like superpowers, and the more of them you have, the more valuable you become. The stronger you are able to build the "I," the easier it is to transform your life into whatever you desire.

Can you imagine if a person was to join five different sports teams within a year and was able to learn the skills of the best players from all the teams? This would enable an individual to become more valuable than a person who is only skillful playing one sport. The experiences from being a member of five different teams will give that individual leverage over someone whose only played with one team. As a public speaker, you should want to learn and know about as many things as possible, that way you can be prepared for whatever it is that you may come across in the near future. Proper preparation prevents poor performance.

Take your time to learn everything you can about public speaking before you make it your profession. Don't move too fast and expect too much of yourself. Haste makes waste. The way you are reading this book one chapter at a time is the same way you have to approach life: one day at a time. Make sure each day counts. Choose to get up, show up, and never give up on making your dream come true. The people in your life all play a part in the lessons that you will need to learn in order for you to advance.

Be a silent team player if you have to. Admire others from afar while watching their techniques to learn how to implement their style into your own life. Become an outspoken advocate on issues concerning education, health care access, affordable housing, senior citizens, veterans, immigration, economic development, school safety, LGBTQ rights, domestic violence, animal cruelty, and gun violence.

There is an Alternative to Violence Program (AVP) that is ran in some New York State prisons by representatives of the Quakers. AVP has a section called the "I message." It is a tactic used in conflict resolution.

The way it works is: you express how you feel about a situation. You keep it on the "I." For example, by starting the conversation with, "I feel when you yell at me I am unable to think straight. I would like for you to not yell at me anymore." This message forces the other person to come out of themselves and step into your shoes. This same strategy can work in the public speaking realm because any time you are able to get others to understand where you are coming from, they will be more willing to accept your message. The "I" message works in more ways than one. Not only do you get to let others in on who you truly are, but you also give them an opportunity to find the connections between themselves and you. There are many ways to begin, but only one truly works.

You start by telling *your* story. Dig deep into your heart and come out with everything you've got. When you come from the heart, your audience will feel you and connect with you on a more personal level than if you had just read from a piece of paper or teleprompter. Speaking from the heart is the difference between reading a typed letter and one that is handwritten. When you speak about yourself, people will listen to see if they too have experienced some of the same trials and tribulations as you. When they do come across some similarities between their lives and yours, it will make them feel closer to you and much more acceptable of your message.

Telling your audience your life story is all about connections, making the story relate to your message and your audience. If you can find a way to include your audience in the story, you will win them over. Imagine you're telling a story to a basketball team about how devastating it felt when your high school home team lost a game to the visiting team. Every basketball player in the room will be able to relate to that story in one way or another.

You can end the story by telling your audience how you felt on that day after that happened, and then go around the room and ask if anyone here has ever experienced losing a game. I can almost guarantee everyone will have their hands up, ready to tell you about how they felt the first time they, too, experienced losing a game. This is one of the best demonstrations of finding the "I" in team. To take a sport that is played by a group of people, then to individually get the perspective of each player, automatically makes you an honorary member of the team.

Individuality is like a priceless gem that everyone wishes to possess, and many do. But it is only valuable when recognized by those who know its worth. To recognize it is to place a spotlight on its possessor and allowing them to shine while standing amongst their equal. Have you ever wondered why, at the beginning of any basketball game, the team will line up and (one after the other) an announcer will call out each of their jersey numbers along with the name of the player? I believe this is done to place the spotlight on each individual as a reminder that although you are part of a team, you are mainly responsible for the "I." So, when it's crunch time and the game is on, all eyes will be on you watching to see what it is that you're going to do that's different than everyone else around you.

Jen: "Ohh my God! Joe, that felt so good."

Joe: "What? The foot massage? It was only—"

Jen: "No—I mean, yes—no, I mean... The foot massage was great, but I was referring to chapter nine. It felt good to know that I am not being selfish if I decide to take part in something for the sole purpose of benefiting myself. Especially when what I'm learning is something that can be beneficial to others in the long run."

Joe: "I guess I don't have to ask you what have you learned. I was hoping you'd give me the chance to ask, and I was also hoping you'd say that you've learned I give a great foot massage."

Jen: "I'm sorry, Joe. Go ahead, ask."

Joe: "Thank you. What have you learned?"

Jen: "Well, I've learned that you give a great foot massage."

Joe: "Thank you. It was my pleasure. What else?"

Jen: "And that your hands feel amazing."

Joe: "Okay, and what else?"

Jen: "And that sometimes the best way to overcome the fear of speaking in public is by participating in sports, volunteering to do community service work, or any extra-curricular activities that allow you to socialize, analyze, and vocalize your opinions within an organized group setting."

Joe: "Jen?"

Jen: "Yes, Joe?"

Joe: "Marilyn Monroe couldn't have said it better. It's amazing the way you grasp everything and regurgitate it all with the basic understanding of a school teacher."

Jen: "All thanks to you, Professor Joe. You make it all so simple."

Joe: "As it should be. You see, Jen, that is the magic of *Speaking Potion*: it's simplicity. People make things hard to comprehend when they are trying to hide something or be able to change its meaning, interpretation, when it no longer benefit them. That was one of the reasons why I dropped out of law school. The truth was always changing with time."

Jen: "I know what you mean, Joe. I'm a straight shooter kind of gal and I guess that's why *Speaking Potion* appeals to me so much. I had fun reading chapter nine. Can I read chapter ten, too?"

Joe: "You sure you're up for it?"

Jen: "Of course! Why wouldn't I be?"

Joe: "Did you read the title of chapter ten yet?"

Jen: "No, but I'm about to flip the page right now."

Joe: "If you're going to do it, you have to do it in your Marilyn Monroe voice again."

Jen: "Okay, but only if you read the last two chapters in Bill's voice."

Joe: "Bill Gates?"

Jen: "No."

Joe: "Bill Cosby?"

Jen: "No way!"

Joe: "Bill Deblasio?"

Jen: No, no, no. Bill Clinton."

Joe: "Bill Clinton!"

Jen: "Yes, Joe, Bill Clinton."

Joe: Okay, fine, but then you will have to be Jennifer Lewinsky."

Jen: "Who's that?"

Joe: "Monica Lewinsky's better-looking half sister."

Jen: "Just for that, you're getting Hillary... After her second election."

· CHAPTER 10 ·

TOOL SHED

What's in your tool shed? If you had to take inventory of everything you've learned throughout your life that is beneficial to you becoming a great public speaker, what would you consider to be your best tool? Is it your voice? Your ability to remember things? Your looks? Your level of education? Your financial status? The goals you've accomplished? Your family, friends, and associates?

All of the above are vital tools that you can use to further your career as a public speaker. Overall your life experiences are the most valuable tools in your shed. Everyone has been through certain things in life that are worth speaking about with the rest of the world. Everyone has a story to tell. Your tool shed might be filled with tools that can help someone get through a bad marriage to an abusive spouse. If you've been through it and made it out alive, you are now equipped with the necessary tools that can be passed on to help out a multitude of people.

Having a tool shed is having experience, knowledge, and wisdom, and understanding/knowing the value of all that you possess. Life is filled with people, places, and things that are broken. It is all of our responsibilities to use our tools to help make the world a better place. If you are a farmer, your knowledge of agriculture is your tool. It is a valuable tool that many people depend on in order to survive. If ever you were to decide not to harvest your crop, many people will go hungry and die. So your tool, although it may be naturally embedded in you, is meant to be shared.

It is meant to benefit others as much as it benefits you. Should you choose to stop being a farmer and instead give lectures to others on the art of farming, you would still be serving the same purpose as if you were still farming. Being a public speaker is one of the only professions that *anyone* can get into. As long as you have something to speak about, there will always be a crowd of people to listen.

Some people might not believe that to be a factual statement. If you consider how big the world is and the billions of human beings who inhabit the earth, it is not hard to conceive that groups of people may want to learn what you naturally know. There is no such thing as a worthless tool shed. I strongly believe we all have something within us that is valuable to others. No matter who you are or what you've been through in life, there are people out there who will value your life experiences.

In accordance with Darwin's theory of survival of the fittest, we can not evolve until we learn to master our environment. Say ten people are left on an island where you have to know how to swim in order to hunt for food. Only two are swimmers. If the two who are swimmers don't teach the eight who can't swim, there will soon only be two survivors left. Knowing how to swim was a tool that, if not shared, would cause eight lives to disappear. This is why a person who is fully engaged in the affairs of his or her environment will always have the upper hand: the most essential tools in his or her shed. And as a public speaker, *you* are already equipped with the necessary tools in your shed to get you started and place you ahead on your journey. You probably have so many tools in your shed that you can't even think which is the most valuable.

To find your most valuable tool, we will have to dig into your shed. You might find the perfect tool to use to build yourself the perfect public speaking career. Are you ready to start digging into your tool shed? Great! Before we start rummaging through your private property, I need you to understand that the phrase "tool shed" is a metaphor for your mind and all of its contents. Your mind is the shed and the tools are your thoughts. All of your life experiences are locked inside of your tool shed. You store your tools in the shed to keep them from getting damaged, lost, or stolen.

The way we tend to separate or compartmentalize our everyday tools from our emergency-use tools is the same way we tend to treat our thoughts, feelings, emotions, and responses. Depending on the situation at hand, we either deal with it accordingly or habitually. In the scenario of the ten people left on the island, dealing with that situation accordingly would be for the two that know how to swim to teach the eight that don't so that they all as a collective would've survived and lived longer. Dealing with the situation habitually resulted in the two swimmers remaining as the only survivors.

Using your very own life experiences, if you had to give a speech on an event in your life that impacted you the most, what would your speech be about? Who would want to listen to it? Who would your speech benefit and why? Your habitual response might be to speak on an event that left you emotionally devastated or one that made you financially successful. Either way, your tool shed has everything you'll need to navigate through life without having to depend on outside influences.

Everything you'll need in order to survive or to better your life is inside your tool shed. You have all of the solutions to all of your problems. There is nothing in life that will happen to you that you won't be able to handle. Everything that you break you have the ability to fix. Every word that you speak has the ability to build or destroy. You are the creator of your world, the master of your life. The same way you choose who and what to love or hate, is the same way you can choose who and what to fear. I choose to fear nothing and no one but God.

To have fear of speaking in public is to fear your fellow men. Human beings who bleed like you, sleep like you, eat the same food and breathe the same air as you. Why would you allow your equals to have so much power over you? Can they cause you to melt from staring at you for too long? Are their eyes not made from the same substances as your own? Can they cause you to die from shouting obscenities at you while you're speaking? Are their voices made of stones? No. So why would you choose to fear something that is only but a replica of yourself? Do you fear or love yourself? If you love yourself, reciprocate that feeling towards your audience.

Reciprocating is a tool in everyones shed. We all have access to it and the ability to use it to our benefit. Whenever you're on a stage, behind a podium, or in front of a large crowd speaking, you have to remember that *you* are in control. Not them. The same good energy you feel towards yourself and your message should be reciprocated to your audience immediately in order to set the tone for your presentation. You can use a smile, joke, quote, or any other effective tool in your shed you deem to be valuable.

You can raise the value of every tool in your shed by making sure that they remain sharp and useful. You have to master each and everyone of them by not allowing your tools to control you but instead you have to remain in total control over them. You have to know what purpose each and everyone of your tools serves. You have to know what's in your tool shed, and be capable of using every tool you have at your disposal.

Life is hard for most people, but if we prepare ourselves properly, sooner than later life will become easier for us to navigate through. Being aware of our naturally possessed tools can help us to make better decisions in life. We just need to work with the miracles we were given and allow ourselves to accept our position in life's big puzzle, instead of trying to place ourselves in places where we don't fit. We were all created with certain talents, skills, abilities that are essential to our self-preservation. Aside from these innate gifts, our environment has equipped us with the ability to add more tools to our shed. Through our life experiences we've accumulated enough knowledge of the world to become the president of our very own company. If each and everyone of us harnessed our energy, we can all soar to great heights of achievement.

If becoming the greatest public speaker in the world is your ultimate goal, you can achieve it if you focus enough energy into what's required and how to utilize what you already possess. It all starts and ends with you and you alone. No one else can do for you what you need to do for yourself. If you fail at this mission, it is because you choose not to believe in your ability to overcome your fear of public speaking. If you had to speak to a group of prisoners every day in order to feed your family, would you be able to do it, or would you allow your fear to cause your family to die?

I know that might have sounded harsh, but it's the reality for people that are public speakers. Any day, you might be confronted with a task that requires you to talk or walk. You can't afford to discriminate when it's time to put food on the plate. Believe it or not, you are a business. Any time you can be compensated for anything that you do, it's considered a form of business. As a public speaker, you are now a company.

Let's say your current age represents the amount of years your company has been in business. For that amount of years, would you say you've been running a successful, profitable business? If your knowledge, talents, and skills were to be employees of your business, how many employees are you currently utilizing? In other words, how many tools does it take to operate your business? Hopefully, you've been using every tool available in your tool shed to develop and expand.

In the world of public speaking, you will have to take a similar approach. Everything you've come to know and learn you will have to continually put to use. Why? Because if you don't use it, you will lose it. Once you've developed your public speaking skills it is like growing muscles. Just like weight lifters exercise their muscles to maintain strength, health, and physical appearance, a public speaker must always be ready, willing, and able to jump at any opportunity to speak. Use one or all of the tools in your public speaking tool shed. We have to utilize many different tools in our lives to get certain jobs done. Just like plumbers and mechanics. One of the most valuable tools for a public speaker is his or her mouth. Similar to how a race car driver has to maintain his vehicle in top shape, public speakers must maintain their skills.

You want your teeth to be shining their whitest and your breath smelling listerine fresh. Since your mouth is one of the main tools that you will be using to speak from, you should invest in the best toothpaste on the market Everyone appreciates a speaker with fresh breath, especially if the speech is given in a confined room under extremely hot temperature. The mouth is a public speaker's golden goose. Each speech given can be the equivalent of a golden egg. You should want to protect your investment at any cost. If possible, get a contract with a dentist because you never know when you will have to take your mouth to the shop for a tune up.

As your communication tool, your mouth should always be kept hygienically proficient. Your lips should remain moisturized, not cracked or chapped. If you have facial hair, keep yourself groomed at all times, especially whenever you're in public. You're whole body is a representation of you as a public speaker, so you want to make sure that you look your best at all times. Keep your fingers manicured in case someone hands you a microphone to hold while there are cameras in your face. No matter what it is that you might be speaking about, if your nails are dirty that is the only thing that most people will focus on and remember. You want to always leave everyone with a good impression of your overall character.

Depending on the route you wish to travel with your public speaking career, you might want to get into the habit of studying the dictionary to learn and retain new words. Vocabulary is an essential tool to possess. The more words you know the meaning of and how to properly use them in a sentence, the more intelligent you will appear. But you don't want to just appear intelligent—you want to actually become more intelligent.

Set the standards high for yourself. As you aim to reach the next level of achievement, challenge yourself along the way. Your mind is filled with different ideas from your life experiences on how to turn anything around you into a useful tool. You might not be able to see them now, but once you start looking, you will come to find tht whether from nature or your nurture, you possess a unique set of experiences that only you can explain. There is a story in everything. For every story, there's an audience.

If you're a person with the memory of an elephant, then you should have more tools in your shed than a Home Depot. If you're someone whose done a lot of drugs and alcohol and can't seem to remember what you had for dinner last night, then being a public speaker might not be for you—unless you are willing to put in hours reading your speeches so you can remember them for when you will have to give a presentation (or if your speeches are going to be about being an addict, than all you'll have to do is talk).

Most people use their tools to fix things that are broken, and in your tool shed are all the tools you need to fix the things that are broken in your life, community, relationships, and the world. Imagine if everyone knew they had the power to change everything around them for the better just by speaking about the problem and listening for the solution. One time a friend of mine had a problem where he was bleeding from his rectum after having a surgery. As embarrassing as this may sound, he shared it with me nonchalantly. About a month later while reading a law magazine I came upon a story where a man was awarded $1.5 million from a law suit relating to malpractice that resulted in rectal bleeding. I gave my friend a copy of the article and he was elated because he suffered from the same injuries and was now able to be compensated.

Jen: "Wow! Thanks for showing me your tool shed. I'm surprised."

Joe: "Well, most guys don't like showing ladies their tool shed. I can see why you're surprised. But what I want to know is—"

Jen: "What have I learned! Well, Master Sensei, I've learned that my life experiences are the most valuable tools in my shed. And that everyone has been through certain things in life that are worth speaking about with the rest of the world. Life is filled with people, places, and things that are broken. It is all of our responsibilities to use our tools to help make the world a better place."

Joe: "Hey, Jen, you alright? Why are you crying?"

Jen: "Because that was so beautiful. When I read the chapter, I felt like everything you wrote spoke to my heart and made my insides get all mushy. I just wish more people can see things like you and I do. The world would be a better place."

Joe: "You know the best way to make a difference in the world is to first start with yourself and lead by example so that others can follow you until they are able to become leaders of their own. This is why I wrote *Speaking Potion*: to plant the seeds in the soil so that one day multitudes will be able to eat from the fruits."

Jen: "There are a lot of hungry souls out there, and I don't mean hungry in the physical sense. More like a hunger for knowledge, wisdom, understanding, and most importantly, the hunger to know ones true self."

Joe: "Jen, those who don't know their true self are people who are scared to look within. If anyone wants to know who they truly are, all they have to do is analyze the things they love to do and within those things, they will find themselves."

Jen: "I want to share everything I've learned so far from *Speaking Potion* with the world, Joe. Your book has transformed me into a different person, a better person. A fearless and much more passionate individual. I really appreciate your help. I couldn't have made it this far without you."

Joe: "Of course you'd have made it. You were born to do this. It's people like you who make an impact in the world through your passion for helping others and bettering yourself. I commend you for being the strong women that you are. Without women like you, there would be no men like me. I'm only a success at what I do because I have friends like you who support my ambitions."

Jen: "But I could never be as successful as you, Joe."

Joe: "Why not?"

Jen: "Because I'm not as good with words. I have very strong feelings for a lot of things, but expressing how I feel in writing is not one of my strong points."

Joe: "Jen, once again—"

Jen: "Let me guess, I said something to help your transition?"

Joe: "Yes. Chapter eleven is about exactly what you're in need of. I will go through the process with you and help you understand why it is important to know what you want your speech to be about. If you understand the importance of your topic of choice and you are passionate about it, guess what?"

Jen: "What?"

Joe: "You've already written your speech. I didn't think you'd be ready so soon, but you've proven me wrong. You were determined to overcome your fear of public speaking and have taken the necessary steps to make that happen. For that I say....'

· CHAPTER 11 ·

LET'S WRITE A SPEECH

Congratulations! you made it to one of the most important chapters in *Speaking Potion*: "Let's Write a Speech." This is where you are going to utilize everything you've learned to write your very own speech. Don't worry, I'm not going to let you do it alone. We are going to write it together. Are you excited? You should be. This speech will determine whether you are ready for the world of public speaking—or do you need to read this book over again so you can get a better understanding of everything you've read?

Remember, you are not alone in this. We're going to do it together. We are going to start from everything you've learned from chapter one up to now. If you've been paying attention, writing your first speech will be easy. I will use the most simple format to get you started. Before we start, I want you to take a second to think about the answer to this question: Do you understand why it is important to know what you want your speech to be about? If you understand the importance of your topic, you've already written your speech. Now all you have to do is keep up with the mechanics of a basic speech outline.

Starting a speech is like starting Kindergarten. Do you remember your first day of Kindergarten? When you walked into that classroom full of new faces, the first thing that was requested of you by the teacher was to introduce yourself. As a rule of pleasantry, it is always better to greet your audience before introducing yourself. So a simple, "Good evening ladies and gentlemen" should always be at the top of your introduction. When you open with recognizing your audience, it forces them to reciprocate by recognizing you.

Now that you've got their attention, it's time to introduce yourself: "My name is_____." Make sure that when you announce your name, you say it loud enough for everyone to hear. I once was at a conference where the guest speaker stated his name as the audio technician was tweaking the microphone, and the microphone's volume went down for a brief second. When the guest speaker was done speaking and it was question and answer time, not a single person was able to address him by name. That took a lot away from him building his reputation because he was a great speaker, but no one remembered his name.

So, make sure you clearly state your name after you greet your audience members. The next thing you will need to do is create an attention-grabber. Depending on what your speech is about, you can use a quote, ask a rhetorical question, create a scene by using a scenario, tell a joke—but only if you're 100 percent sure you'll get a laugh out of everyone in the room—or make a declarative statement like I did in my speech, "Time to Rise:" "By the time I'm done speaking, many children across the country are going to die."

That's a bold statement to make. Let's see what opening we can come up with for you: "Good evening ladies and gentlemen.

My name is Jennifer. I am going to show you how to use your mouth to make a million dollars."

Beautiful! Now that's one of the best attention-grabbers I've ever heard. Everyone wants to be able to make more money. Everyone has a mouth. By appealing to a person's financial desire, and letting them know that the only tool they will need is one that they already possess, you've just gained the attention of everyone in the room. Congratulations!

You've just covered the first three parts of your speech. You've greeted your audience, introduced yourself, and used an excellent attention=grabber. Now you have to tell them what it is that you will be talking about and why they should believe you. If making money and helping others make money is your passion, then you shouldn't have any problem talking your talk.

Assuming you watch and learn from others and are able to apply the correct copycat effect, which should be you being your 100 percent authentic self, all you have to do now is connect your passion. You should be ready to talk about how a person can use their mouth to earn a million dollars and why you are the right person for them to be hearing this message from. Ready? Let's do it.

"Good evening, ladies and gentlemen. My name is Jennifer. I am going to show you how to use your mouth to make a million dollars. This is a simple method anyone can use. All you have to do is find a product you use every day and do some research to find out how many other people use this product. If there are over a million users, contact the company that makes the product and offer your service as a salesperson for a percentage.

Once you become an employee of the company, you can build a website to sell the product using a drop mail service so you won't ever have to even stock the product. Create videos of yourself talking about using the product and get other users of the product to log onto your website. Offer them discounts for purchased items. The reason why I know this is a proven method is because after reading *Speaking Potion*, I created a webinar of myself reading chapters from the book over the internet. I generated over a million views and was able to get a million copies of *Speaking Potion* sold."

Joe: "Jennifer, you are a genius. That was beautiful. Not only did you manage to capture my attention, but you just gave me an idea."

Jen: "Yeah, what kind of idea did I give you?"

Joe: "I think I'm going to take what you just said into consideration. I mean, it makes perfect sense."

Jen: "What makes perfect sense, Joe? Come on, tell me. I mean after all, it was my idea, wasn't it?"

Joe: "Okay, okay, fine. I'll tell you. Are you ready?"

Jen: "For God's sake, Joe, yes. Just tell me already."

Joe: "The Speaking Potion Challenge."

Jen: "Speaking Potion Challenge?"

Joe: "Yes. The Speaking Potion Challenge."

Jen: "How does that work?"

Joe: "Simple, Jen. Simple. For everyone who purchases a copy of *Speaking Potion*, he or she will get a chance to win money through generating views."

Jen: "How do you mean?"

Joe: "All a person has to do is video tape themselves reading a chapter of the book or multiple chapters of the book and whoever generates the most views will either win a certain amount of money or request it be donated to a charity."

Jen: "And anyone will be able to enter the Speaking Potion Challenge?"

Joe: "That's right, anyone. As long as they have a mouth."

Jen: "So even a five-year-old can enter the contest'?"

Joe: "Of course a five-year-old can enter! Even a ninety-five-year-old."

Jen: "Sweet! I think I'll be the first to take on the Speaking Potion Challenge. So, let's finish my speech."

Joe: "Okay, being that you have covered so much in such a little time, we won't repeat what you've already done. The only things left are your specifics, which are the two main points that you will cover about your topic, the body of your speech, and finally the conclusion. With the conclusion, you will have to show your audience how your two points connect with each other. Then tell your audience exactly what you need for them to do after hearing your wonderful speech.

Jen: "Okay, I think I got this. No, I know I got this. So far I've connected my passion and I recognize who my audience is, and because they are my potential future customers or clients, I shall cater my two points to their needs."

Joe: "Go get 'em, tiger! You can do it."

Jen: "Was that your way of calling me a cougar?"

Joe: "I would never. What I meant to say was *show me the money*."

Jen: "So, ladies and gentleman. In my quest to show you the money, there are two points I would like to present to you. One is the "magical motion of the mouth," and the other I like to call the "tactics of technology." I will show how using these two extremely effective devices can change a person's tax bracket from an apartment renter to a home owner. From an Uber Driver to a Lear Jet traveler. You won't need any money to start, but you will have a whole lot of money when you finish. The techniques that I'm about to teach you will enable you to build a network of influential contacts and leverage them for your own benefits. Some might say this is the key to success, and if it is, then you are already very successful because you naturally possess everything that is required of you for you to achieve this new level of wealth that I'm about to reveal to you. It's an old family secret."

As powerful as a lot of our modern forms of communications may be, there is nothing as powerful as the word of mouth. Speaking about the benefits of something and getting others to want to go experience it is the most effective marketing strategy there will ever be. Unlike a written letter or an electronically sent message, word of mouth travels with substance. The sound of someone's voice speaking can be desirable and hypnotizing to the listener. Now add an actual human being to the equation, preferably an attractive man or woman, and the experience can be something magical.

The magical motion of the mouth is a tool that is equipped to convince or control a group or individual. Ones point gets across much more effectively when face-to-face with an opposing party than if a letter or text was sent. A person's senses are awakened when interacting, whether on a business or personal level. As the mouth is moving to speak, the listeners eyes are watching the speaker as if a physical component of the words are ejecting out of his or her mouth. The speaker's voice causes the listener's ears to activate as it filters the message to the brain to be processed and prepared for a possible response.

All of those motions cause ones body to remain energized, and in turn produce supplies of endorphin that help to create feelings of emotional attachment to the speaker. You then become a willing servant, as you pass on the message to the next person, all while experiencing a euphoric sensation that creates a sense of power, knowledge, wisdom, and understanding. You can now get anyone to say or do anything once they are captured by the magical motion of your mouth. I was able to implement this method into my videos to create a large following fan base.

Once I gained some followers, I began to apply some tactics of technology. Although I'm not too internet savvy, I watch enough episodes of *Ridiculousness* to know that people like to be entertained by watching others make a fool of themselves. So I created a website called www.Speaking-PotionPranks.com*. The site catered to internet videos of people making a fool of themselves. I convinced all of my followers to upload any funny videos that they come across onto my site to be rated by one another.

Again using tactics of technology, I implemented a lottery system where I gave out prizes to readers of *Speaking Potion*.

*SpeakingPotionPranks.com is mentioned only for entertainment purposes and, to the author's knowledge, does not exist at the time of publication.

All a participant has to do is register their receipt number and where the book was purchased to be eligible to win. The more people who register, the bigger the prizes, and I made sure to build a special section on the site just to display all the winners with their prize. Some people won money, cars, clothes, jewelry, phones, tablets, concert tickets. The best thing is that these things were given to me freely by sponsors that wanted nothing in return but to have their company promoted through the SpeakingPotionPranks website.

I was able to build a lucrative network using the magic motion of the mouth, to convince people to go buy the book and to share its contents with others. Tactics of technology enabled me to create a bigger platform, using the magical motion of the mouth of others to provide opportunities while entertaining my audience. You, too, can achieve the same level of success using many of the products that are already out on the market. Whether it be books, toys, cars, electronics, music, food, clothes—you can turn anything into something spectacular by speaking about it and getting others to speak about it, too. The more people you get, the bigger the profit.

As a business person you will have to know how to talk to people about buying your product. You have to be able to tell them why it is that your product is better than its competition. The reason why I sold so many copies of *Speaking Potion* is because I was passionate about the whole idea of sharing the information in the book with the rest of the world. I understood the importance of making sure that the book was read, discussed, and put into practice by everyone who had a fear of speaking in public.

I was on a quest to make *Speaking Potion* a New York Times Best Seller, and I accomplished my goal. I strategized every step of the way as I watched, listened, and learned from the best authors. Once I understood their strategies, I used the copycat effect to make their methods of success work to my advantage. I believed in my product, so talking my talk came naturally when it was time to apply the magical motion of the mouth. I recognized my audience enough to know what to tell them, what they wanted to hear, and how to say it in a way to make them comply, go out, and buy.

In my webinar I was able to communicate all of this to my audience, whom I had come to consider to be a part of my team. I let them into my tool shed and, in return, they reciprocated. I was able to utilize some of their tools to develop my own unique set of motivational incentives. As more sells of the book started pouring in, using my method my viewers begin setting up their own accounts to sell products for some of the companies that are being promoted on my website. We supported each others ventures and were able to align. By coming together it made it easy for us all to become successful, because as a rule of gratitude we remained connected as a network in order to allow the benefits we reap to circulate within.

Without the power of *Speaking Potion*, I would not have had the ambition to make any of this possible. I would not have known that I can use my mouth to become a millionaire. You, too, have what it takes to make *millions* of dollars, if you choose. You can prosper in whichever field you place your energy into. You don't have to go through life hoping things will one day get better for you. You have the power to make things better for yourself *right now*.

Stop depending on others to do for you what you can do for yourself. A closed mouth can't eat, so speak up. Open up about the things you love. Speak about the things you believe are right. Speak about what's going on in the world and how you perceive it all with your eyes. Speak about all lives and why they matter. Speak about the unusual changes that are constantly happening with the weather. Speak about the world and what it will take to make it all better.

Use the magical motion of your mouth to speak to everyone you meet, whether inside of a crowded elevator or the street. Be free of judgments, spread yourself as wide as the sea. Use tactics of technology to get across boundaries, break barriers, create unity. Show the world how to turn their fear into their fortune. Open your mouth and let your every word become a speaking potion. Devote yourself to your passion. Dedicate your time to the action of things that are beneficial to your audience. Train yourself to treat everyone as if he or she is the most important. Do for others as you would do for yourself, never more, never less. Surround yourself with people that have your best interest at heart. Always aim to finish everything that you start, and let every word out of your mouth come from the bottom of your heart.

Joe: "That was beautiful, Jen. I think I'm in love."

Jen: "In love?! With me?"

Joe: "Nooo! With your speech."

Jen: "Ohh!"

Joe: "What's the name of it?"

Jen: "The name of it! I don't know... The Love Potion."

Joe: "Beautiful, yes. The love potion speech. I like it."

Jen: "I thought you said you loved it? Now you only like it? Men!"

Joe: "What I love, Jen, is the fact that you are so creative you were able to come up with a speech about my book, using all of the chapters we read through. You are amazing. I think I want to hire you to help me promote it."

Jen: "Wow! This must be my lucky month. First I get offered to be a spokesperson for Vain Apparel, and now you're offering me a job to promote your book *Speaking Potion*. What's next?"

Joe: "Contracts, of course. You know, the legal stuff."

Jen: "No, no, I mean. You know how they say good things comes in threes?"

Joe: "Oh! Well, this is the city that never sleeps, so you never know. You might come across a movie deal before the night is over."

Jen: "Movie deal?! Nooo! I don't think I'm ready for that. I'm just learning to overcome my fear of public speaking and now you're talking about me being ready to act in a movie?!"

Joe: "But of course, Jen. You can do anything you put your mind to. You're young, beautiful, smart, and have a great personality. I mean, if I ever get the chance to turn any of my books into a movie, I would want you to star in it."

Jen: "Really? You would *really* want me to star in your movie?"

Joe: "Why wouldn't I? After all, the world is your stage. Being that you've come this far, I believe you are ready."

· CHAPTER 12 ·

THE WORLD IS YOUR STAGE

Now that you've proven that you're determined to possess the power of *Speaking Potion*, get out there and speak. The world is your stage. Never again shall you be afraid. Fear is nothing but **false expectations appearing real**. Take control of your destiny and turn fear into **future expectations appearing real.** Your future expectations of being a public speaker will make you smarter, more attractive to the opposite sex, more capable of influencing others to do good deeds.

Your newly acquired public speaking talents will open doors of opportunity for you and put you in places amongst people who are generous, wealthy, intelligent, creative, kind-hearted, connected, and great. There are people who've paid hundreds of thousands of dollars in schools, such as Harvard, Princeton, and Yale just to obtain degrees of studies that aren't compatible to their passions. You, on the other hand, have paid less than $20.00 for a book of priceless information that can place you ahead of any college graduate. *That* is the power of *Speaking Potion*.

Now that you're in possession of it, you must pass on the knowledge of its existence in order to create the necessary flow of energies, to cause the intended effect in the hearts and minds of the rest of the world. Leave no men, women, or children be-hind. We all have a story to tell that the rest of the world needs to hear. Lets spread our message and give voices to the voiceless. No longer shall *you* remain silent and in fear of speaking your mind. You have a voice, use it to fight for justice, peace, and equality. Let not your heart be troubled. Speak up for those who can't speak for themselves. Use your voice to help feed the hun-gry, shelter the homeless, protect the weak from their prey. Use your speaking ability to lead the way.

Your voice is a tool that can bring others pain or pleasure. Choose to use it for good, and help make the world better. You are a treasure. No longer buried, but found. Your words can heal wounds. Your voice can create actions and move mountains. The world is your stage, and you are its star. The things that you say can cause you to stagnate, or take you far. The choice is yours and it will always be. You are made to be a winner. Open your eyes and see. Set your mind free. Now is the time for you to come out and be all that you can be.

The world is your stage, and stage time is all the time. Pre-pare your speech, so that your every word remains in your mind. Greet your audience with a smile, and use gestures that are kind. Maintain eye contact with all. When you speak use the power of fours. Never give the audience your back as you walk across the floor. Use your charisma and charm to turn a cold audience warm. Get the crowd to participate, ask them questions about things that they can relate to. Know when to take a break, pause after speaking a long sentence. If anyone is sleeping make them wake up. Use the power of your voice inflection.

The world is your stage, you are now a champion. Use repeat-ed phrases, and in your listeners mind your message will sink in.

The world is your stage, never show any fear. You can build your self-confidence by working on your memorization. If you speak they will listen. Be precise and be clear. Use your respiratory system correctly to make your words glide elegantly through the air. The power that you are able to conjure through your breathing, is strong enough to move a crowd of over a million.

Now is your time. So take heed to the signs that are all around you. Understand that you have a passion that is powerful enough to propel you to the top as a public speaker. Watch, listen, and learn from the best, and allow them to become your teachers. Indulge, don't deny yourself. Use the copycat effect to acquire the skills you desire. Talk your talk and let your walk be the proof. Speak your truth with the innocence of a youth.

Connect with your passion so that the correct changes in your life can began to happen. Use *Speaking Potion* as your navigation as you travel through different dimensions to deliver your message. Get to know your audience, command their attention, use emotional and or logical appeals. Keep it real. Control your lips, mean what you say and say what you mean. Don't use deception to try to paint a false sense of perfection. You already have everything it takes to become great. You're astrologically connected to many men and women who've already made it. You are an extension of them.

Breathe easy, keep on going until you make it to the finish line. You don't have to rush things, you can take your time. If learning slow is what will help you grow, then by all means, take it slow. Read the book over one chapter at a time. Keep on reading it until you have it all in your mind, locked in, ready to recite at the drop of a dime. Keep it on the "I" and do the things that you need to do in order to better yourself. Put yourself first in everything you do and do it to the best of your ability. Raise your living quality through the use of your oratory skills. Speak until your public speaking fears are dead. Use your powers of eloquent words to mesmerize your listeners minds.

The world is your stage, and your experiences are your stories. Like fables of old times, stories are meant to be repeated and past on from generation to generation. Stories are tools of the mind. Like all tools of the mind, if you don't use it, you will lose it. There is certain information from your life experiences that can be essential to the survival of a family member, friend, or a neighbor. But most importantly, that information is critical to your very own survival. That is why they are stored in your tool shed. By now you should have understood the concept of a tool shed to know how valuable your experiences in life are.

I'm sure you've accumulated enough tools through out your life to have an abundance of valuable knowledge on demand. You are a commodity and a self-owned corporation. You do not need anyone to give you a hand out, you don't have to walk around in life with your head down. If you do, sooner or later your whole body will go down. Like the stock market when it crashes. If you can understand that you are a business, like everyone else in the world, it is now up to you whether this business succeed or fail. Your tool shed is filled with products that you can use to gain financial wealth.

I've come to believe that there are three kinds of people in life: get-overs, workers, and business owners. The get-overs are the ones that grow up to become burdens on taxpayers, the workers are the taxpayers, and the business owners—well, they rule over the workers and create laws to control and punish the get-overs. We all have it in us to become business owners, even those of us who are get-overs. All it takes is to come to the realization and understand that we are all naturally born wealthy. Our value derives from our experiences, which are worth more to others than they are to ourselves. The world is your stage, speak about your experiences.

Where are you currently in life? How did you get there? Speak about it. There are many people who are trying to get to where you are right now. Market your experiences to them. There are many people who are trying to avoid landing in the same position as yourself. How did you get there? What mistakes did you make to wind up living such a horrible life? Market your experience to them. You have an audience. We all have an audience. As humans we are and always will be each others audiences. If you can market one of your many experiences to cater to a specific group of people, you can become a successful business.

Speaking Potion is more than just a book to help you overcome your fear of public speaking. It is written to help you look at life from a different perspective—an alternate view to help create an alternate *you*. A "you" that you will look at in the mirror and be proud of. A "you" that others will look towards for advice and up to for inspiration. A "you" that will know the secret to success is to first invest in yourself. You invest in you when you face your fears. Be willing to change. Be willing to learn. Be willing to think and act different than you normally do when faced with the same scenarios.

When you invest in yourself, your health starts to get better. You are now eating healthier food, your body looks and feels stronger. You are now exercising, practicing yoga, running, jogging, getting pedicures, manicures, haircuts, facials, massages, meditating, dancing, rock climbing, canoeing, swimming, and doing things to keep your body in motion. As your mind begins to expand, you become sharper, wittier, like a well-oiled machine. You are ready to take on any job that is presented to you.

The world is your stage. There is no need to fear what others may think of you. Most people you will come across in life will not be a permanent fixture. You are the star of your show. They are nothing but extras who've come to fill a small part. Some are there to make an impact or pass on a message. Regardless of this, you are still the main character in your life. When it's your time to shine, you have to make sure that you shine the brightest. The same way you sometimes have to play an extra in the life of others, they sometimes play one in yours. Know the difference so that you won't allow an extra to outshine you. Be prepared at all times to take total control of any situation where public speaking is involved. You never know when you might have to save a fellow public speaker who's drowning. Be bold whenever you are presented to be the guest speaker at functions. Use all of the tools you've learned from *Speaking Potion* to wow your crowd. Keep up with the news, fashion, current events, music, entertainment, and new laws. You want to be able to always analyze yours and other peoples thinking, opinions, and beliefs.

The world is your stage. Stay in the state of recent, be in the now. Whatever it is that you want to use your public speaking powers to do, become the greatest at it. Read everything that you can find on your specific interest. Study it. Get in touch with others that are already in that field. Interview them like I've done in the process of writing *Speaking Potion*. You'll be surprised to see how happy you can make someone by asking them to share with you some of the tools in their own tool shed. People want to be recognized for doing the things that they're good at. When you show interest in someone else's craft, that gives them a sense of purpose.

It gives them a sense of pride and sometimes the motivation to keep going at it. If a person refuses to share their knowledge of a common interest with you, that is not someone you should want to invest your time in. Only invest your time and energy with those who will help you to grow. I'm sure you didn't just read all twelve chapters of *Speaking Potion* to put it down and forget about all of the wonderful jewels you've come across. It would be a waste of time and energy, you would receive no return on your investment. As a business, prosperity should be your number one goal.

You have the power to now transform your life. You are one person in a world of billions of people with the understanding that overcoming the fear of public speaking will open the flood gates to finding solutions to many peoples problems. The best way to better ones position in life, is by helping others. You can choose to become the voice for the voiceless, or teach the power of *Speaking Potion* to them and help them develop their own voice so that they can speak up for themselves.

Communication is an essential tool to help keep people connected. But like the Tower of Babble, we've been brought down and divided in order to keep us from reaching certain heights in life. When I read that story in the Bible I understood it to mean that when you do things with the wrong intention, anything you gained will be taken away. So, in your effort to bring people together, make sure that you are doing it for all the right reasons. You will be greatly rewarded when the time is right. Don't let greed cause you to forget where you came from or who you are. Public speaking can catapult your life to the extent where you're being paid thousands of dollars for speeches that last less then twenty minutes. Don't lose yourself.

Don't allow the amount of money you're being paid to make you forget about your morals and principals. Many people are going to try to use your speaking ability for their own self-interest. Some might want to pay you large amounts of money to help them sell products that you don't agree with. To speak on a topic that you don't believe in. When faced with such moral dilemmas, the best thing to do is take a pause and think about the situation. Give yourself enough time for yourself to truly listen to your heart to see if this is something that your mind and body is comfortable with. You will know because there will be signs like, butterflies in the stomach, doubts, indecisiveness. When these moments occur it is better to turn down a lucrative deal, than to take it on knowing you aren't being real to yourself.

This is why I propose that you only do the things that you are truly passionate about. Achieving goals of subjects that are close to your heart, is the best feeling of success one can ever get to feel. No amount of money can match the feeling of knowing that you have truly made a difference in the lives of others. To know that you've helped an entire community with their problems of homelessness, hunger, crimes, violence, poverty, unemployment, obesity, bullyism, drug addiction, alcoholism, or whatever it is that you may be passionate about. Its the best feeling in the world.

As a matter of fact, I challenge each and every one of you that owns a copy of *Speaking Potion* to commit yourself to using your newly acquired power of public speaking, to go out there into your community and find one problem that touches you and fix it. Use the power of your speaking potion to build an internet based community of other like-minded individuals to help you with your goal.

I believe you, too, have it in you to use the power of *Speaking Potion* to begin to do great things in the world. You are a powerful being who possesses the ability to cause supernatural things to happen. Not just in your own life, but also in the lives of people whom you have not yet met. You are on the right path towards your calling in life. If you choose to stay on this path, you'll be rewarded with all that you deserve and more. Like a domino effect, it will happen for myself and everyone else that owns a copy of *Speaking Potion* and puts the lessons into practice as a daily curriculum in their lives. This is not Voodoo. This is something greater than magic: it is *you*.

You have the power to transform your life right now at this very moment if you are willing to believe in yourself and the energies that are vibrating within your mind, body, and soul. This is all happening in your life. It is *your time*. There comes a time in everyone's life when we come to realize that we must evolve. In order to make the necessary transitions, we acknowledge that there are some things that we need to learn before we can make it to the next level.

Overcoming your fear of public speaking is one of those things you needed to learn. Now to learn how to swim, you have to jump in the water. To become good or great at speaking in public you have to *speak* in *public*. To answer the question from the introduction: *that* is why I joined the theater workshop. I wanted the opportunity to speak in public, overcome my fear, prove to myself that I'm able to do anything I choose to put my mind to. And so can you, my friend. So can you.

Jen: "Thank you so much, Joe. I think I got it now. I'm ready to go face my fear. I understand now: to become great at speaking in public, I have to speak my truth. I have to feel passionate about something that is worth speaking up for, and I know what that is."

Joe: "How do you know?"

Jen: "I know because as I was listening to you it came to me. I feel it. It was like a moment of clarity that awakened the deeply buried secret I've been hiding for years."

Joe: "What is it?"

Jen: "Well, Joe, before I share that with you, I need to know two—"

Joe: "Alright, alright, alright, I'll tell you about the little girl, Michelle."

Jen: "What about the favor you need?"

Joe: "You're here, aren't you?"

Jen: "So that was the favor you wanted? My company?"

Joe: "Yes! I love having you around, Jen-Juice. And plus, after your break up with Mr. Not-So-Nice-Guy, I thought it might be a good idea for you to spend some time with people who really care about you and have your best interest at heart. I'm delighted to have you with me right now."

Jen: "Thanks Joe, that means a lot to me. I appreciate you."

Joe: "Show me how much you appreciate me?"

Jen: "How?"

Joe: "Well, you can start by closing your eyes."

Jen: "Okay. My eyes are closed."

Joe: "Now take a deep breath, as I'm about to whisper into your ears what I need you to do."

Jen: "What did you say?"

Joe: "I said, Jen, what have you learned? And tell me with your eyes closed."

Jen: "I learned that being a public speaker will make you smarter, more attractive to the opposite sex, more capable of influencing others to do good deeds. Public speaking talent will open doors of opportunities and put you in places amongst people who are generous, wealthy, intelligent, creative, kind-hearted, funny, connected, and over all great company."

Joe: "Well, Jen, the world is your stage."

Jen: "And however I choose to express my artistic side the world will oblige. As long as I come from the heart."

Joe: "I wish I had a certificate to give you, Jen, 'cause you sure are a potential certified public speaker."

Jen: "So you really think I have it in me?"

Joe: "Yes. Everyone does. Everyone. Especially those who don't think they do. All it takes is a flip of the switch to turn the mind from thinking that it can't to it *will*. You, Jen, I know you *will* become one of the greatest public speakers. What you've showed me tonight is that it's in you and you are ready to let the world feel the impact of your passion."

Jen: "Oh, you're such an excellent motivational speaker. I feel like you can make me open your window right now and fly out of this luxury building."

Joe: "Well, Jen if you do, make sure you don't land on the entrance to the Barclays Center. The Brooklyn Nets have a game tomorrow and I would hate to see this building all over the news for the wrong reason. And if you're going to jump, at least don't do it without first allowing me to steal *this* from you."

Jen: "Oh God, Joe. I haven't been kissed like that since high school."

Joe: "Is that why you puckered your lips like a blow fish, and kept your eyes closed?"

Jen: "Yes, no, maybe so. I mean, I don't know. All I know is I feel like your tongue just released a Voodoo virus on me. But before I forget my name, can you please tell me what happened to the little girl, Michelle?"

Joe: "Oh yeah, that's right. Michelle. Well, using all of the music and dancing DVDs I gave her, Michelle went home and copied all the moves of the dancers, sung along with the singers, and by the time the talent show came around, she knew how to dance like a young Jennifer Lopez and sung like Beyonce."

Jen: "Wow! So did she win?"

Joe: "Not only did she won the competition, she also received a recording deal from a well-known record label and is now currently touring overseases with her chart-topping number one hit song. Oh, and her father, well, let's just say he now has more ties than he will ever need."

Jen: "Wow! Joe, I guess Michelle found her passion through using the copycat effect, huh?"

Joe: "That's right. And um, Jen, I want to thank you for your help."

Jen: "My help! With what?"

Joe: "My new book."

Jen: "What book is that?"

Joe: "Kissing Potion."

Jen: "Kissing Potion! What is it about?"

Joe: "Getting to first base without striking out."

· CONCLUSION ·

Since you were able to get through all of the twelve chapters without giving up on yourself, congratulations! You've completed my twelve steps of public speaking. Now you can go out there and motivate and captivate the world. Don't be afraid of what anyone will think or say, as long as you say what's in your heart, people will see that you are smart, attractive, caring, passionate, real, motivated, and ambitious. People will be at a loss of words to describe you. Fear shall no longer be a factor in your life. Well, at least not the fear of speaking in public.

When you apply the speaking potion formula in your life, your verbal inadequacies will slowly start to diminish and your outlook on the challenge of speaking in public will change. As mines have. I had to begin to recognize that my insecurities were brought about from my fears. I had to begin to see these fears not as a barrier, but as an obstacle to rise above. It was only then that I came to truly believe that my deepest fear was not that I was inadequate. My deepest fear was that I was actually powerful beyond measure, that is why I was able to participate in the theater workshop and stayed on until the completion of our final performance. If you want to overcome any fear in life, you have to be willing to face it. Those false expectations appearing real will no longer be a hindrance.

The courage it takes to face a crowd of strangers and speak comes from being passionate about the topic. Speaking in front of a crowd is a challenge, only when you don't have a clear understanding of what your goal is, and aren't connected to your overall message.

The basis of *Speaking Potion* is to supply you with tools to enhance your ability to speak in front of any crowd without having the fear of not being in control of your actions. When you speak, you are sending out energy to the listeners, and controlling the flow of energy is essential to your message being delivered correctly, and coherently. Each chapter of *Speaking Potion* is designed to help you harnessed your powers, so that you can effectively disperse all elements of your speech.

From understanding why you want to be a public speaker, to actually stepping on the world stage to speak. Each process must be filled with passion and authenticity. When you are in tune with your message, your body will relax and allow you to deliver effortlessly. That is the power of speaking truth into existence. Nothing gets in the way: no stuttering, no sweating, no forgetfulness. No one can ever ask you any questions that will make you feel uncomfortable, as long as you are speaking *your* truth. Own it.

I understand that we are living in a time where people are offended quickly and are very sensitive to what they hear. Don't let that stop you from speaking your truth. As you can see, even our president Mr. Donald J. Trump gets under people's skin sometimes by the way he says or responds to certain things. One would think that as the president of the United States, he should have a filter on his speech. But, because he doesn't, people trust that he means what he says. So no matter how one may feel about the man on a personal level, logically you know what you are getting from him is the raw and uncut truth. His truth. Some choose to buy it, others don't. That's just the way of the world. You, too, have an audience waiting to hear your truth.

If you're choosing to cater to your audience, be prepared for all that is to come. Keep *Speaking Potion* close by so that you can use it as a reference whenever necessary. Know that you must be passionate about your topic if you want others to understand you and take you seriously. Watch, listen, and learn from all that is around you in order to perfect your craft. Learning from mistakes made by others, prevents you from making them, too.

Don't be reluctant to borrow from others. There is nothing new under the sun. The qualities that you may admire about one person, usually is a re-invention that was taken from someone else. Bring your own style and pizzazz to things when using the copycat effect, and all people will see is your originality. Especially if you are talking your talk while doing it. Speaking from your heart and allowing others to get to know the real you will win them over all the time. The ones that you don't win over? Don't worry about them. They were never meant to be won over by you, anyway. Focus your energy on those that are receptive to your message. Plant your seeds and allow them to grow. Convert your passion and remain connected to the people, places, and things that makes you happy in life.

Recognize the fact that your audience matters. Feed off of each others energy. Remember that your body is a temple, keep it clean and stress free. Align yourself with like-minded individuals and take as much from them as you are able to give. Get out of your shell and become a team player if you want to increase your value. Keep your tool shed filled with sharp tools. I believe many readers of this book will go on to accomplish great things in life. Hope to hear you all and see you all on stage. I'll leave you now to check out my speech, "Time To Rise," along with a couple of interviews from two great public speakers I came across. Enjoy!

TIME TO RISE

Good evening, Mr. Toastmaster, fellow speakers, and audience members. I am Colby Sylvain, and by the time I'm done speaking, **many children across the country are going to die.**

Today I would like to speak to you on the importance of recognizing bullyism and standing up to it. Has anyone in here ever bullied someone or been the victim of a bully?

According to the Center for Disease Control and Prevention, 4,400 kids commit suicide every year, some from being bullied. How many of you here would be willing to help lower that number?

Martin Luther King Jr. once said, "To be a witness to an injustice and not doing anything about it, makes you just as guilty as the one committing the unjust act." As strong men and women we should not sit idle while the children of our future are killing themselves. **It's time for us to rise!** So today, there are two very important points I would like to present to you. A virus called hate and a cure called love. One is a gift, and the other is a curse. Which one will you choose to fight against bullyism?

Bullyism has become a disease that's infecting every sector of our great nation. From our government officials to our next door neighbors. I believe to eradicate bullyism, we must all first recognize the bullies within ourselves. Bullying comes in many forms: verbal harassment, physical threats, blackmail, cyber threats, prejudice, psychological manipulation, inequality, oppression, injustice, racism, slandering, slick-talking, friendly extortion, intimidation, gossiping. The list goes on, ladies and gentlemen.

Every day around us people are being bullied. Whether it's a female because of her feminine vulnerabilities, gay male because of his homosexuality, or an immigrant because of his ethnicity. What this all boils down to is hate. We all have hate for something or someone. And bullyisn is nothing more than the hate manifesting into actions. If you've ever disliked someone because of their; weight, height, complexion, occupation, race, religion, financial status, sexual preference, gender, mannerism, mental illness, physical disability, physical appearance, or simply for your own personal reason. Then *you* my friend are infected with Hate that can one day turn into bullyism. **It's time to rise above it all!** Every day in communities across our nation, children are being bullied. In schools they're being taunted, tormented, and tortured by their peers, because of the color of their hair, the clothes that they wear, the homework they've *done*, or the group of kids that they've shunned. Being a victim of bullyism can be traumatizing, turning ones life into a terrifying experience. Imagine your child waking up everyday to deal with feelings of anxiety, depression, and rage. The depression can cause kids to commit suicide, turn to alcoholism, and or drug addiction. While the rage can cause them to shoot up their school, place of worship, or get locked away in a prison cell or mental institution.

As a society, we've paid little attention until recently. As you all may have witnessed through current events, bullyism is at an all time high. That means the hate virus is spreading like wildfire. It's becoming an epidemic that is threatening to deteriorate our government, communities, but most importantly it is destroying us.

Our elected officials use of hatefilled rhetorics has caused disunity amongst us. Law enforcement officers that are infected with hate have caused mothers to become childless and neighborhoods to turn into riot zones while businesses discriminate against minorities and immigrants, causing families to be left hungry and homeless. How long will we allow this hate to persist?

As long as this disease called hate is within our hearts and minds, it will disperse throughout the universe until we are all infected. Until we are no longer able to show love, mercy, empathy, generosity, bravery, humanity, and unity. Bullyism has brought so much pain to so many people that sometimes it takes a miracle or a chance to look at the world from a different view, in order to see the bully within you.

I'd like to share a quick story with you all on why I stopped being a bully. How I got cured of the hate that was in me....

About ten years ago on Christmas Eve, as I was crossing the Brooklyn Bridge coming from Manhattan on my way home from work, I came upon a group of young boys that were tormenting a small, defenseless puppy for their own pleasure. They kicked the puppy around and yanked on its tail and legs. They thought their action were humorous. One of the boys picked up the puppy by its collar and held it over the edge of the bridge, and then shouted to his friends, "Hey fellas, let's see if this mutt can swim!"

The helplessness of the yelping puppy reminded me of the many victims whom I'd bullied in order to get a laugh, impress my peers, boost my self-esteem. As the puppy's body began to convulse while suspended in the air, I knew I had to intervene. So I ran over to the boys and yelled: "Hey! Thank you for finding my lost dog."

Panting, while holding onto the guardrail, I'd reached them in time to have grabbed the puppy from out of the boy's hand. The group ran off laughing and shouting obscenities. As I walked off carrying the puppy in my arms ('cause it couldn't stand on it's own), he licked me in the face, slobbering me with saliva. To this day I believe that puppy's saliva melted all the hate I had in my heart and replaced it with love. In a sense, saving that puppy's life was the best gift I'd ever received. The gift of love.

What is love? Love is the greatest experience in life-but most importantly love is a state of mind that doesn't judge. Love doesn't bully, love doesn't hate. Love doesn't oppress, manipulate, or discriminate. We learn how to love by the culture in which we are raised. We grow up learning about love through watching the interaction with our family, friends, neighbors, and strangers. Our environment helps to shape our understanding of love.

For example, some people say they love; money, drugs, sex, cars, clothes. But *most* of those things we can live without. They are merely distractions that keeps us from loving ourselves and our fellow men. To love is to unconditionally accept yourself and others, no matter the flaws. When you allow love to consume you, hate will no longer have the power to ruin you, because in a heart filled with love there are no room for hate, and where there's no hate, there's no bullying. As human beings we have come too far in life to allow some minor differences to set us back, break us apart. We have to learn to embrace each other's differences, because lets face it, without those differences the world would be a very boring place to live in. If you are a true men and women of God, there should not be any hate in you.

The Bible gave us the cure for the hate virus, in Matthew 22, Verse 39 it states: "You shall love your neighbor as yourself." Now if we all were to follow that one basic instruction, the world would be free of wars, poverty, prejudice, oppression, injustice, racism, hate, and bullyism.

So in conclusion, I ask you all here today to stop turning a blind eye to what's going on around you, and within you. It's time to rise above hate and eradicate it by spreading love amongst one another. You and I have the power to propose, persistent, proper social behaviors in order to profess what it is to be humane.

So let us all make a pledge here today to choose to rise above the people, places, and things that are holding us down in the dumps. Lets all rise together as one, to get rid of the hate in our blood and replace it with love. If you won't do it for yourself, at least do it for the children. They are our future: presidents, doctors, teachers, lawyers, farmers, police officers, veterinarians, law makers, and next door neighbors.

Everyone of you who is capable of showing love, have the power to end bullyism. Love is like knowledge: to keep it to yourself is to change *you*. But when you reciprocate it you are able to change the world. By you all being here today, listening, you have already taken the most important step towards making a change, making a difference. Now lets all unite to end bullyism by spreading love. Thank you for listening.

Thank you, Mr. Toastmaster.

INTERVIEW 1 WITH A PROFESSIONAL PUBLIC SPEAKER

1) What is your name, and age?

Nathaniel J. I'm in my 40s.

2) How did you get into being a public speaker?

That started in Ciphers, at a very youthful age, being in the setting of others and speaking in general.

3) Did you ever have a fear of speaking in public, and if yes, how did you overcome it?

I watched and observed others in a public setting, whether they are on TV or in person, and I learned from them. I was looking to see whether they appeared to be nervous, and if they were, how they handled that.

4) Were you ever nervous when you first started as a public speaker? If yes, what tactics did you use to overcome the nervousness?

Yes, I was nervous. When I first started speaking I was with a group of men in a political science setting. There were around eight of us and I was terrified. I was giving the authority to run the class that evening so I just took charge. I delegated authority, had one person do the opening, another change the setting. The men didn't question my status they knew I was knowledgeable, and by them being confident in me, I became confident in my self.

5) Have you ever given a speech, if yes how do you prepare?

Yes I have. It depends on whether it's an educational speech or a presentation. If it's educational I do research. I prepare differently. If it's a presentation then the group is there for something and what ever they're there for then that's what I based it on.

6) What tips would you give to someone that have a problem remembering things?

Index cards and practice. The index cards should be minimized with information, but they should have key elements from the presentation so that the elements automatically trigger parts of the presentation. And practice, go over the index cards so that a single card triggers a specific thought.

7) What would you say is the hardest part about being a public speaker, and how do you make it easy?

It's the audience. You have to win them over. I wouldn't call it the hardest part. I would say the greatest challenge. If you say the hardest part then you may be off peaking yourself. Some people do it with humor, some may engage the audience with questions. Sometimes it's a question of interest the majority of the audience can relate to. I believe all of those are ice breakers. When you engage the audience they become part of the presentation, they are no longer just speculators.

8) What advice would you give someone who is interested in becoming a public speaker but has a fear of speaking in public?

I would suggest they concentrate on their presentation, not the audience. I would also suggest when they look into the crowd look at the last row, not the first or the second because the last row encompass the entire audience. Stay focused with your presentation nothing else should interfere with that. If possible, engage the audience because that takes the spot light off of you.

9) For someone who is not a peoples person and doesn't like to socialize with others, is it possible for that person to become good at public speaking?

Those character traits are not necessarily a requirement or standards to be meet. A person's works tells about his thinking, because if it's books, talk shows, radio broadcast, those are his thinkings he may not be a peoples person. His love for his people may be expressed through those venues. This is how we define his worth. Actions and works should always corresponds.

10) Who are some of your top five famous public speakers and why?

1: Martin Luther King Jr. It was his level of disciplined, his focus and his fate. He was a religious man and I believe his faith inspired him to take on all challenges.

2: Malcolm X. Malcolm appreciated his audience, as far as the media and the overall public, he appreciated their aggression and it only inspired him.

3: Al Sharpton. He is eloquent in his speaking pattern, topics and his confidence. When he is engaging the audience I believe it's with defense of the people. Any person that speaks for the people must understand peoples position and society's hipocrisy.

4: Jesse Jackson. Jesse, in my view, I feel he is confident and he himself was inspired by Martin Luther King Jr. I believe he was conditioned and trained, and he watched Martin Luther King Jr. as an example.

5: Barack Obama. Obama came from a grassroot foundation; he's a people person. He walked the streets, he socialized with the people. He went from a street organizer to a college professor, to a Senator, and eventually a President. His speaking is imicable and articulate. He's an eloquent speaker.

INTERVIEW 2 WITH A PROFESSIONAL PUBLIC SPEAKER

1) What is your name, and age?

William King, I'm 38 years old.

2) How did you begin getting into being a public speaker?

Well, the last facility I was at, they didn't have a lot of program. I meet a young man, he was actually older than me about 30 years. He said to me, "I got a public speaking class, why don't you join it." I said sure. I never knew I had a talent for it until I got involved.

3) Did you ever have a fear of speaking in public, and if yes, how did you overcome it?

I still do actually. My hands start to shake. I really never overcame it. I just find that point in time where I dig deep down inside of myself to gather up my courage and face my fear.

4) Were you ever nervous when you first started as a public speaker, if yes what tactic did you use to overcome the nervousness?

Deep, solid, slow breaths before I speak, and I also realized that the key to becoming a public speaker without fear is to know exactly what your talking about.

5) Have you ever given a speech, if yes how do you prepare?

Yes I have, that's one of the requirements for public speaking. Once again to prepare you must be of knowledge of what message or what information you're about to deliver.

6) What tips would you give to someone that have a problem remembering things?

Write down your speech and carry it with you every where you go, so that in your spare time you can recite a sentence or two at a time until its embedded in your head like your favorite song. Also you have to have a passion and a love for the subject.

7) What would you say is the hardest part about being a public speaker, and how do you make it easy?

Being booked at a short notice to speak. To overcome such a thing I found myself using life experiences or stories to compensate for my lack of research time.

8) What advice would you give someone who is interested in becoming a public speaker but has a fear of speaking in public?

They should practice on friends or family gatherings. Tell a few jokes, or get a job that ables them to be more social, where they will have to interact with people. You must be a peoples person in order to be a public speaker.

9) For someone who is not a peoples person and doesn't like to socialize with others, is it possible for that person to become good at public speaking?

Not being a people person can also label you as antisocial, so this would make it difficult for you to get into being a public speaker. Maybe the money would would make you want to try to become someone your not, but I'm not sure if that would be the case.

10) Who are some of your top five favorite public speakers and why?

The author of *Rich Dad Poor Dad*, John Wareham (who is also the author of *How to Fly* and *How to break out of Prison*) and is a Toast Master; Professor Allen Singer of Hofta University; my fellow thespian, Colby Sylvain; and of course, myself are five of my favorite public speakers.

Public Speaking Course

This Certificate is Awarded to

Colby Sylvan

Has successfully completed twenty-one weeks of the Public Speaking Course. He uses the dynamics of public speaking as a catalyst for self-improvement by helping individuals develop better communication methods, elements of listening and social skills. Participants graduate by choosing a personal topic of social and moral importance, researching and practicing it, and then presenting their speech to the general population, guests and staff members.

March 2019

Kathleen G. Gerbing Superintendent

Sponsor, Dan Daly

A. Stevenson Deputy Superintendent of Programs

A. Goldsmith, ORC / Staff Advisor

THE #SPEAKING POTION CHALLENGE

DO YOU HAVE WHAT IT TAKES TO BE AN EFFECTIVE PUBLIC SPEAKER? ARE YOU ABLE TO USE THE TOOLS IN #SPEAKING POTION EFFECTIVELY? WOULD YOU LIKE TO EARN MONEY AS A #SPEAKING POTION REPRESENTATIVE?

If your answer is YES to all of the above questions, take on the #Speaking Potion challenge. You can sign up at www.SpeakingPotion.com or use the referral order form at the bottom. You can make as many copies as you will need. The challenge consist of getting as many people as you possibly can, to read and or purchase a physical copy of #Speaking Potion. Your email address or name and D.O.B. will be used as your referral ID. For every 1000 physical copies sold you will receive a check for $2,000. Receive a FREE copy of #Speaking Potion for every 500 people you get to read the book. To participate in the #Speaking Potion challenge order your copy today.

NAME:		
ADDRESS:		
CITY:	STATE:	ZIP:
REFERRED BY:	REFERRAL ID:	
#SPEAKINGPOTION	$14.99, PLUS $4.99 SHIPPING PER BOOK	
	QUANTITY:	_____ x $14.99
MAKE CHECK OR MONEY ORDER PAYABLE TO:	SUBTOTAL:	
	SHIPPING:	_____ x $4.99
Colby Sylvain	SHIPPING SUB:	
1504 East 95th Street, Suite #1		
Brooklyn, New York 11236	GRAND TOTAL:	

www.ingramcontent.com/pod-product-compliance
Lightning Source LLC
Chambersburg PA
CBHW060853280326
41934CB00007B/1032